Literature in Perspective

General Editor: Kenneth H. Grose

Spenser

To A. D. Rand

With Whom I First Studied Spenser,
This Book is Gratefully Dedicated.

> Which her deep wit, that true harts thought can spel,
> will soone conceiue, and learne to construe well.
>
> AMORETTI XLIII

Literature in Perspective

Spenser

Elizabeth A. F. Watson

Evans Brothers Limited, London

821.3
WAT

Published by Evans Brothers Limited
Montague House, Russell Square, London, W.C.1
© Elizabeth A. F. Watson 1967
First published 1967

Set in 11 on 12pt. Bembo and printed in Great Britain by
The Camelot Press Ltd., London and Southampton
7/5291   44441   PR4136

Literature in Perspective

Of recent years, the ordinary man who reads for pleasure has been gradually excluded from that great debate in which every intelligent reader of the classics takes part. There are two reasons for this: first, so much criticism floods from the world's presses that no one but a scholar living entirely among books can hope to read it all; and second, the critics and analysts, mostly academics, use a language that only their fellows in the same discipline can understand.

Consequently criticism, which should be as 'inevitable as breathing'—an activity for which we are all qualified—has become the private field of a few warring factions who shout their unintelligible battle cries to each other but make little communication to the common man.

Literature in Perspective aims at giving a straightforward account of literature and of writers—straightforward both in content and in language. Critical jargon is as far as possible avoided; any terms that must be used are explained simply; and the constant preoccupation of the authors of the Series is to be lucid.

It is our hope that each book will be easily understood, that it will adequately describe its subject without pretentiousness so that the intelligent reader who wants to know about Donne or Keats or Shakespeare will find enough in it to bring him up to date on critical estimates.

Even those who are well read, we believe, can benefit from a lucid exposition of what they may have taken for granted, and perhaps—dare it be said?—not fully understood.

K. H. G.

Spenser

I have used the one-volume Oxford edition of Spenser's Works (ed. J. C. Smith and E. de Selincourt), for references and quotations. In accordance with my whole approach to this poet, I have tried to give a brief and general bibliography which provides a standpoint from which any specialised interests may be more usefully followed as they arise.

I should like to take this opportunity to make some particular acknowledgements for all the help and kindness I have received in the course of working on Spenser. My debt to Miss K. M. Lea, Vice-Principal of Lady Margaret Hall, Oxford, Mrs. C. M. Ing, Fellow of St. Hilda's College, Oxford, and to the late J. B. Leishman, is of many years' standing. I should also like to thank Dr. and Mrs. Bernard Hamilton for generous help and criticism, Miss Elizabeth Speck and Mr. John France for their help in preparing the manuscript, Mr. Kenneth Grose for his valuable advice and encouragement, and finally my pupils past and present for all I have learned about Spenser through studying his work with them.

E. A. F. W.

Contents

The Author

Elizabeth A. F. Watson, M.A., B.Litt., is Lecturer in English at the University of Nottingham.

Acknowledgements

The author and publishers are indebted to the Goldsmiths' Librarian for permission to reproduce the cover portrait from an oil painting formerly in the Earl of Chesterfield's Library, now part of the Sterling Collection in the University of London Library; Mr. D. L. T. Oppé for the drawing of Charity, and the Trustees of the British Museum for the design for the obverse of Queen Elizabeth's Great Seal of Ireland. The painting of St. George and the Dragon is reproduced by gracious permission of Her Majesty the Queen.

I

Spenser's Importance

It is obvious to any student of English literature that Spenser is an important writer. But because his work has never been in any sense of the word popular, its importance is likely to be seen and described in terms of its influence, particularly on later poets such as Milton, Keats or Tennyson. Having acquired the dubious title of 'The Poets' Poet', Spenser is in danger of being left for poets alone to read, and to judge by appearances it would seem that nowadays even these pass him by. In fact, *The Faerie Queene*, the work by which his reputation must finally stand or fall, is proverbially unreadable. Most people who know Macaulay's famous judgement (in his review of Southey's edition of *The Pilgrim's Progress*, 1831, contrasting Spenser with Bunyan) are also aware of its implication:

> Of the persons who read the first Canto, not one in ten reaches the end of the first book, and not one in a hundred perseveres to the end of the poem. Very few and very weary are those who are in at the death of the Blatant Beast.

Since the Blatant Beast is never in fact killed, it would appear that Macaulay was not himself one of the persevering minority any more than are most of the people who laugh at him for revealing the fact.

Spenser is very far from being unreadable, but there are good reasons, of which the great length of *The Faerie Queene* is a minor one, why he is not much read today. Later in this chapter I shall be discussing some of the outstanding difficulties of his work, as well as trying to indicate how these may be overcome. For the moment, having recognised his importance, I shall attempt to show in what this consists in relation to the literature of his own time: that is to say, what his position is among 16th-century English writers.

Spenser was born somewhere about the year 1552. We can deduce this from a sonnet, probably written in 1593. Here he says that this year, the year of his courtship, seemed to him longer

then al those fourty which my life outwent.

AMORETTI LX

and this would mean that his birth happened within a year or so of the accession of Mary, in 1553. He died, on 16th January, 1599, four years before the death of Elizabeth I. Particulars of his life will be given in Chapter 2; here it is only relevant to notice that it coincided very nearly with Elizabeth's reign (1558–1603), and his most creative years, from 1579 when *The Shepheardes Calender* was published, until his death, with the period which was fullest and most exciting not only in political, international and economic affairs, but also in the literature of the time.

The 'Elizabethan period' has for us today such a glorious association of achievement, and particularly of literary achievement, that it is only by a conscious application of historical knowledge that this appears in a proper retrospect. The achievement is there, but it belongs supremely to the latter half of Elizabeth's reign, and then continues well into the next century, so that in fact, when one speaks broadly of Elizabethan literature, one is usually referring to writings of the last twenty years or so of the 16th century, and very often to those written up to twenty years into the century following. *The Shepheardes Calender* comes in fact at the end of one of the few really blank periods of English Literature: what C. S. Lewis has called 'The Drab Age' of poetry. Spenser himself refers several times to the barrenness of English letters, especially in his early work. Later he inveighs against the lack of reward and encouragement given to poets, but when he himself is beginning to write, he sees every reason also to be depressed by the general decay of talent and inspiration. In the *Eclogue* written for the dreary autumn month of October he sets out his discouragement under four heads: the failure of patronage; the lack of noble subject matter; the inadequacy of the poets themselves and the pernicious influence of fashion:

> But ah *Mecænas* is yclad in claye,
> And great *Augustus* long ygoe is dead:
> And all the worthies liggen wrapt in leade,
> That matter made for Poets on to play:
> For euer, who in derring doe were dreade,
> The loftie verse of hem was loued aye.
>
> But after vertue gan for age to stoupe,
> And mighty manhode brought a bedde of ease:
> The vaunting Poets found nought worth a pease,
> To put in preace emong the learned troupe.
> Tho gan the streames of flowing wittes to cease,
> And sonnebright honour pend in shamefull coupe.

OCTOBER 61–72

He is here citing Maecenas and the Emperor Augustus as examples of true patronage. (The poets Horace and Virgil had owed much to their protection.) Spenser's whole way of presenting his complaint is influenced by an idea common at his time, of which he makes much use elsewhere, that the world was itself in a state of decay, and that it was impossible to match the achievements of ancient times in the modern age. As John Donne puts it, writing in the next century:

> Mankinde decayes so soone,
> W'are scarce our Fathers shadowes cast at noone . . .

FIRST ANNIVERSARIE: THE ANATOMIE OF THE WORLD, 1610

It is interesting that Ben Jonson, writing well into the great literary flowering of the age, says that it is only that 'Men are decay'd and studies. Nature is always the same' (*Discoveries*, first published 1640).

At the time when Spenser is writing thus bitterly, there is nothing in the achievement of his contemporaries or of his immediate predecessors to suggest that the next thirty years, the next half century even, is to be a time of literary glory unparalleled in English or any other European literature. The last notable writers had been Skelton, Wyatt and Surrey. Skelton had died in 1529, thirty years before Spenser was born, and his fame died with him. His scintillating irregularity of diction and metre, his sheer individuality, working outside the most cherished conventions of the new learning which looked for models rather to Rome and Italy than to medieval writing (the conventions of which, whether learned or popular, it despised), ensured that Pope's description of him, 'Beastly Skelton', should express 16th- as well as 18th-century critical opinion of his work. It is only in the present century that his work has been appreciatively revalued. Thomas Wyatt (1503–42) and Henry Howard, Earl of Surrey (1517–47), many of whose poems appeared in *Tottel's Miscellany*, 1559, are in a different position. Both are considerable poets and both went to Italy for new forms and metres. Wyatt wrote the first English sonnets; Surrey the first English blank verse, to mention only their most important innovations. Both are viewed in retrospect from towards the end of the century as pioneers in the 'reformation' of English poetry. George Puttenham, one of the great critical writers of the age, commends them almost entirely from this point of view:

> Who having travailed in to Italie and there tasted the sweet and stately measures of the Italian Poesie as now are newly crept out of the schools of Dante, Ariosto and Petrarch, they greatly polished our rude and homely manner of vulgar [that is, vernacular] poesie, from that it had beene before, and for that cause may justly be sayd the first reformers of our English meetre and stile . . .
>
> ART OF ENGLISH POESIE, 1589

Elsewhere in the same work Puttenham says that he finds 'verie little difference' between Wyatt's poetry and Surrey's, and the reason for this seemingly incomprehensible impression is that for him their technical innovations are the most important thing about their work:

> Their conceits were loftie, their stiles stately, their conveyance cleanly, their termes proper, their meetre sweet and well proportioned, in all imitating very naturally and studiously their Master Francis Petrarch.

Puttenham is writing this ten years after the publication of

The Shepheardes Calender, and in the intervening time Sir Philip Sidney had written his sonnet sequence *Astrophell and Stella*, and *An Apologie for Poetrie*, which had circulated in manuscript though they were not printed until 1591 and 1595 respectively. Marlowe's *Tamburlaine* was written and produced not later than 1587, and published in 1590, and George Peele's pastoral drama, *The Arraignment of Paris*, in which he uses many of the names of the shepherds from *The Shepheardes Calender*, was performed before the Court *c.* 1581. Besides these works, which seem to us outstanding even today, Puttenham is able to speak of the poetry—for the most part then unpublished—of Raleigh, Dyer, Greville, Gascoigne and others.

Puttenham is not here seeing Wyatt and Surrey as originating the new movement, the full current of which is rising even as he looks back to the early years of the century. Rather they are isolated pioneers, whose achievements would not, in that age, have received such elaborate critical attention had their methods not also been those of later writers such as Spenser himself, Sidney, and others. Neither Spenser nor Sidney owed their use of Italian forms, and especially the sonnet, directly to Wyatt and Surrey: they went to Petrarch and to other models. It is only once the new flowering of English letters has truly begun, that these earlier writers can be seen as having gone to the same fertile stock for fresh grafts to transform the ancient native stem. At the time when Spenser, in *The Shepheardes Calender*, is considering his own poetic ambitions in the light of classical and modern continental achievement, there is nothing to mark Wyatt and Surrey, or indeed any other native writers since Chaucer, as worthy predecessors. For Spenser's ambitions go quite beyond the scope of such a form as the sonnet or its conventional subject matter as this had been established by Petrarch and his followers, writing of love in Italy and France. Even as he is writing *The Shepheardes Calender*, he is thinking of it as prentice work. As 'E.K.' says, in the *Introductory Epistle* to the poem, Spenser is here:

> following the example of the best and most auncient Poetes, which deuised this kind of wryting, being both so base for the matter, and homely for the manner, at the first to trye theyr habilities: and as

> young birdes, that be newly crept out of the nest, by little first to
> proue theyr tender wyngs, before they make a greater flyght.

Spenser, that is, is here following the examples of Theocritus and,
above all, Virgil, as well as of modern writers, Italian, French
and Spanish. The point of this is made clear, again, in the
October Eclogue, when one young shepherd, Piers, urges another,
Cuddie, 'in whom', as we are told at the beginning of the
eclogue, 'is set out the perfecte paterne of a Poete . . .', in these
terms:

> Abandon then the base and viler clowne,
> Lyft vp thy selfe out of the lowly dust:
> And sing of bloody Mars, of wars, of giusts,
> Turne thee to those, that weld the awful crowne.
> To doubted Knights, whose woundlesse armour rusts,
> And helmes vnbruzed wexen dayly browne.
>
> There may thy Muse display her fluttryng wing,
> And stretch herselfe at large from East to West:
> Whither thou list in fayre *Elisa* rest,
> Or if thee please in bigger notes to sing,
> Aduaunce the worthy whome shee loueth best . . .

37-47

Spenser's ambition, in fact, is to write a national epic, which will
relate to the history and achievements of the England of his time
as did Virgil's *Aeneid* to the Rome of Augustus.

To Spenser, living and writing when he did, this was not
merely a great but also a very complex undertaking. Many of the
difficulties that his poetry has for modern readers arise from this,
though not all. Perhaps the most obviously difficult thing about
Spenser's poetry, about the way he thinks and expresses himself,
is his use of allegory, and this, with all the many questions that
belong to it, will be the subject of Chapter 3. But before trying
to explain this, before discussing his use of sources, his learning,
the kind of imagery he uses and the range of meaning he attaches
to it, it is necessary first of all to ask the questions that make up
the surest and fairest approach to any artist working at any time.

What is he trying to do? How is he trying to do it? Why is he
trying to do it? Does he succeed in doing it?

It is always necessary to ask these questions, but in the case of Spenser it is perhaps especially important to do so soon, at least as regards the first three, before any serious attempt to read him. The answers are not such as anyone today is likely to find by happy accident. Also, it is easy to be misled, as C. S. Lewis has pointed out in the *Allegory of Love*, by Spenser's reputation as 'The Poets' Poet'. It is easy, happening upon such a verse as this, to be enchanted by its beauty:

Vpon a bed of Roses she was layd,
As faint through heat, or dight to pleasant sin,
And was arayd, or rather disarayd,
All in a vele of silke and siluer thin,
That hid no whit her alablaster skin,
But rather shewd more white, if more might bee:
More subtile web *Arachne* cannot spin,
Nor the fine nets, which oft we wouen see
Of scorched deaw, do not in th'aire more lightly flee.

FAERIE QUEEN II, *12*, 77

But if we linger over this exquisitely sensual description of the enchantress Acrasia, forgetting its place in the whole context of Guyon's quest (Guyon is the knight whose Virtue is Temperance), then we are in danger of becoming ourselves like one of Acrasia's own victims; like Verdant, for example, who is sleeping beside her:

His warlike armes, the idle instruments
of sleeping praise, were hong vpon a tree,
And his braue shield, full of old moniments,
Was fowly ra'st, that none the signes might see;
Ne for them, ne for honour cared hee,
Ne ought, that did to his aduauncement tend,
But in lewd loues, and wastfull luxuree,
His dayes, his goods, his bodie he did spend:
O horrible enchantment, that him so did blend.

FAERIE QUEENE II, *12*, 80

The description of Acrasia is beautiful, and to read it is a delight, but neither the beauty nor the delight are the end of the matter.

15

They have a definite function. By no other means could Spenser have conveyed so clearly the strength of the temptations the enchantress sets before even the noblest knights. Guyon's quest is no easy one. Again, such a passage as this, which describes the serpentine monster Errour defending herself against the Redcrosse Knight, is physically sickening:

> Therewith she spewd out of her filthy maw
> A floud of poyson horrible and blacke,
> Full of great lumpes of flesh and gobbets raw,
> Which stunck so vildly, that it forst him slacke
> His grasping hold, and from her turne him backe:
> Her vomit full of bookes and papers was,
> With loathly frogs and toades, which eyes did lacke,
> And creeping sought way in the weedy gras:
> Her filthy parbreake all the place defiled has.

FAERIE QUEENE I, *1*, 20

The feeling of actual nausea which this arouses in the reader should be the stronger for expressing a moral revulsion. Errour is not just a monster out of a fairy-tale, or a nightmare. She is the first foe encountered by Holiness, who, on earth, is the Church Militant. To Spenser, this meant the Church of England, but this is only relevant for the moment because it means that anything attacking it or its teaching was also an attack on the State, for the Queen was, as is our present Queen, Head of the Church of England. Similarly, treason of any kind was, by inference, also an attack on the true Church of God in England. The 'bookes and papers' are interesting: this is a reference to an actual outbreak of seditious pamphleteering, but that is by the way. To Spenser, error, intellectual error, is not a question of disagreement or even of being mistaken. He views it, in the particular instance, in this case of the Roman Catholic Church of his time, as being inseparable from its conclusions, as we today may think of Naziism as inseparable from its consequences in Belsen or Auschwitz.

Both these passages are sure of provoking a reaction, and a reaction that is at least a part of the whole effect intended, or in tune with it. This next verse, which in its context is equally important, would have received an equally ready response from the kind of reader Spenser himself had in mind; such a man as Sir Philip Sidney, or Sir Walter Raleigh, for example, who had had the benefit of the kind of education which will be discussed in Chapter 2.

> The frame thereof seemd partly circulare,
> And part triangulare, O worke diuine;
> Those two the first and last proportions are,
> The one imperfect, mortall, fœminine;
> Th'other immortall, perfect, masculine,
> And twixt them both a quadrate was the base
> Proportioned equally by seuen and nine;
> Nine was the circle set in heauens place,
> All which compacted made a goodly diapase.
>
> FAERIE QUEENE II, 9, 22

This is part of the description of the House of Alma, that is, the human body, inhabited and governed by the soul. It is an extremely difficult stanza, and its various implications have been worked out at length by Alasdair Fowler, in a way quite fascinating for anyone with a mathematical turn of mind (*Spenser and the Numbers of Time*, Appendix I.) Here, in view of what Spenser himself has said, it is only necessary to point out that the castle is shown as having a framework divided according to two fundamentally different 'proportions', which correspond to the rational part of man, his mind, and to his passionate part, the body, respectively. The 'quadrate' which is the 'mean' or meeting place of the two, expresses the integration of these two component parts in a perfectly balanced personality.

Quite apart from the fact that Spenser here assumes a range of knowledge in his reader which he would be very lucky to find today, he is also expecting a kind of response for which the natural capacity is as rare as the talent of an infant prodigy for chess. The effect of the stanzas previously quoted was sensual and emotional, and by these means they were intended to react upon the intellect. Here the reverse should be the case: it is the intellect that is appealed to, and its response should act in turn upon the emotions. For, by this arithmetical elaboration, Spenser is presenting the idea of Order, of perfect balance and harmony in the universe, and above all, in Man, who of all the Creation should most truly exemplify its potential perfection in all respects, being made as he is in the image of the Creator. Spenser in fact is here making almost the same point as when, in a sonnet to his beloved, he calls her:

> The glorious image of the makers beautie.

AMORETTI LXI

The pleasure to be obtained from reading Spenser is not merely an intellectual one: the first two stanzas quoted go to show that clearly enough, and even this last example expects a wider and richer enjoyment. It is, however, fair to say that for a true appreciation of his work the activity of the intellect can never be totally suspended. Even though it may be forgotten in the imaginative response to some great flight of allegory, it must be ready to apply this to the whole context that is to be illuminated. I shall say more about this in Chapter 3. Meanwhile, we have only partially answered our first question: What is Spenser trying to do? Give a very complex and varied kind of enjoyment to his reader? Certainly, but to what end? This question can best be answered by stating Spenser's own requirements for the great national poem he desired to write.

First of all, it must be a national poem. It must glorify England, as a national power, and as the seat of royalty, of honour, of nobility. It must use native traditions, not only of subject matter, such as history and legend, but also of language, if not of form. Spenser would not even have taken for granted that his great poem was to be written in English: it was a matter for decision. It might have been written, like Petrarch's epic poem *Africa*, in Latin, as being the only language fitted by usage for such a work. But he chooses English, because this is to be in every sense an English poem, and one purpose it has is to establish English as a language equal, in literary power and achievement, to Italian, and even to Latin and Greek. It was to these languages that he looked for models for the form of his poem; this will be gone into in more detail in Chapter 3. But for the language, he has, as we have seen, no immediate models in his own country. He looks back, in fact, to Chaucer for whom he has already expressed his love and admiration in the *June Eclogue*:

> The God of shepheards *Tityrus* is dead,
> Who taught me homely, as I can, to make.
> He, whilst he liued, was the soueraigne head
> Of shepheards all, that bene with loue ytake . . .
>
> Nowe dead he is, and lyeth wrapt in lead,
> (O why should death on hym such outrage showe?)
> And all hys passing skil with him is fledde,
> The fame whereof doth dayly greater growe.

81–4, 89–92

He does not attempt to write Chaucerian English, but he does adopt a deliberately archaic diction, as a way of expressing his sense of the continuity of the traditions of English poetry on the one hand, and on the other, giving his work the authority of ancient sources of subject matter and of style. (Virgil sometimes includes deliberately archaic reminiscences of much earlier Latin poets for this latter reason.) Nor does the fact that his models include Virgil and Ariosto, among others, detract from the thorough-going patriotism of his method, for English will only prove itself on the terms of the very greatest models, by challenging them, as it were, on their own ground. This goes a long way towards answering the next question: How does he try to write a great national poem? The answer is far more than a matter of language of course. Once the decision to write in English was made, the kind of diction he was to use was determined as much as anything by his attitude towards the great poets of all ages, writing in all tongues. These were his models, because they had fulfilled an ambition like his own, and because, like any writer of his time, Spenser believed that to show a rich debt to the greatest writers was to ennoble his own work; to give it authority. His is an inclusive method; nothing that is of value to his purpose is debarred. It is a magnificently courageous approach, and demands much of the reader. As will be shown in Chapter 3, there are many effects in his work that depend on an allusion to or paraphrase of another writer, such as Ovid or Virgil, being precisely recognised.

But how is he to present England as an ideal kingdom, which it plainly was not, and Elizabeth's court as the seat of all honour, virtue and beauty? Spenser had no illusions about the actuality:

> To loose good dayes, that might be better spent;
> To wast long nights in pensiue discontent;
> To speed to day, to be put back to morrow;
> To feed on hope, to pine with feare and sorrow;
> To haue thy Princes grace, yet want her Peeres;
> To haue thy asking, yet waite manie yeeres;
> To fret thy soule with crosses and with cares;
> To eate thy heart through comfortlesse dispaires;
> To fawne, to crowche, to waite, to ride, to ronne,
> To spend, to giue, to want, to be vndonne.
>
> MOTHER HVBBERDS TALE 897–906

He solves this problem by setting his poem in Faerie Land because here he can show the truths that are his real subject matter, undistorted and unmarred by the world as it is. He addresses the Queen:

> And thou, O fairest Princesse vnder sky,
> In this faire mirrhour maist behold thy face,
> And thine owne realmes in lond of Faery,
> And in this antique Image thy great auncestry.
>
> FAERIE QUEENE II, Prol. 4

By using allegory so as to allow of particular topical allusion, he is able to tie his poem down to fact just as much as he wishes, without being hampered by it. Errour, for example, is the foe of Holiness in all times and places, not merely on the particular occasion of the spread of a group of scurrilous pamphlets which were produced by Roman Catholic exiles attacking the Queen. So Glory is always sought by the Magnanimous, the completely virtuous man, or so Aristotle said, as Gloriana is sought by Prince Arthur. But Elizabeth is Gloriana, and can be Gloriana without irony, because the compliment lies in the fact that she has *suggested* Gloriana to the poet. She is the 'patterne' for such perfection, as he says elsewhere in the poem:

20

But where shall I in all Antiquity
So faire a patterne finde, where may be seene
The goodly praise of Princely curtesie,
As in your selfe, O soueraine Lady Queene,
In whose pure minde, as in a mirrour sheene,
It showes, and with her brightnesse doth inflame
The eyes of all, which thereon fixed beene.

FAERIE QUEENE VI, Prol. 6

Behind this high compliment, and behind the whole allegorical method of the poem, lies the idea, which derives from Plato, that Beauty, and the Good that is one with it, is, like all other qualities, so diffused in the real world that the most beautiful woman, or the best action, can only *suggest* the true, undistorted, undiluted nature of these qualities themselves. The 'mirrour' in fact here gives a truer vision than mere sight or factual representation. I shall have more to say about this in the course of the next two chapters.

Why then, is Spenser doing all this? Certainly, he wants to establish English letters on an undeniable equality with those of the classical world and of contemporary Italy and France. So much has been said, but it begs this main question. Perhaps the best way of approaching the answer is to take Spenser's dedication to the first three Books of *The Faerie Queene*, published in 1596:

TO THE MOST HIGH, MIGHTIE AND MAGNIFICENT EMPRESSE RENOVVMED FOR PIETIE, VERTVE, AND ALL GRATIOVS GOVERNMENT ELIZABETH BY THE GRACE OF GOD QVEENE OF ENGLAND FRAVNCE AND IRELAND AND OF VIRGINIA, DEFENDOVR OF THE FAITH, &C. HER MOST HVMBLE SERVAVNT EDMVND SPENSER DOTH IN ALL HVMILITIE DEDICATE, PRESENT AND CONSECRATE THESE HIS LABOVRS TO LIVE VVITH THE ETERNITIE OF HER FAME.

This is Spenser's public declaration of his purpose, and of himself. Because he is a poet, he has a duty to use his talent not merely for private entertainment, or for the expression of his own thoughts and feelings, but in a public capacity, as he might a talent for the law, or, as he in fact did for many years of his life, his aptitude as a civil servant. The idea that a man should use his abilities in the service of the State, and use them responsibly, is central to Renaissance ideas of education and government, as will appear in the next chapter. Here a distinction must be made. Men like Sidney and Raleigh wrote poetry, but their primary obligations, by birth and training, were to the government of the country. Sidney actually feels at times that his love for Stella, which is his great inspiration for poetry, is a distraction from what should be his prime concern.

Certainly, such poets did not think of publishing their verses; they might circulate them in manuscript among their friends, but that was all. Nor did they try, or wish to try, to write a poem of the scope of *The Faerie Queene*. Spenser, like all his contemporaries, regarded poetry as complementary to the deeds, or the virtues it celebrated, or, in the case of love poetry, the beauty and charm. For poetry conferred fame, even immortality. It is an idea that is expressed over and over again in poetry of this period. So Shakespeare writes:

> Yet, do thy worst, Old Time: despite thy wrong,
> My love shall in my verse ever live young. . . .

SONNET XIX

and thus Spenser offers his great poem to Elizabeth 'to live with the eternitie of her fame'. So great a Queen is not dependent on his labours, as might be the case if this were mere love poetry, written to a private woman. Her name will live anyway, but because Spenser has presented to posterity the image of her perfected court in Faerie Land its ideal spendour is reflected forever on the actual woman, the actual Queen. And because Spenser can give this gift of 'maiestie diuine' (*Faerie Queene* I, Prol. 4), the fame bestowed is mutual, the privilege of giving and receiving it, reciprocal. To the 'eternitie of her fame' Spenser and his poetry are indissolubly bound.

2

Spenser's Life

The most interesting facts about the life of any great writer are
those which help his readers to understand his work. In Spenser's
case this is particularly true, for the influences on his poetry of his
education, his friends, and his work as what would now be called
a civil servant, are all important. It is doubly true, because all
three are interesting in themselves, quite apart from Spenser. His
school was the Merchant Taylors' School, one of the newest and
most advanced seats of education in the country. His friends
included Sir Philip Sidney, the Earl of Leicester and Sir Walter
Raleigh. He was a student at Pembroke Hall (now College),
Cambridge, at a time when it was a particularly lively centre of
religious dispute. And as secretary to Lord Grey in Ireland, he
was personally involved in one of the most controversial, as well
as one of the most turbulent, political situations of his age. It is
impossible to give even a brief outline of his life without touching on nearly all the major social and political issues of his time.
He was the kind of man who was naturally inclined to take a
prominent part in the affairs of his age. As we saw in the previous
chapter, Spenser regarded his poetry as having a public function:
as contributing to the glory and grandeur of the State in a way
directly complementary to the rule of the Queen and her
ministers.

SPENSER'S FAMILY AND EARLY CHILDHOOD

We know very little of Spenser's family and circumstances. He
was born in or about 1552. His father has been identified with a
certain John Spenser, a gentleman, whose family and home were
originally in the Pendleton district of north-east Lancashire. He

had moved to London, however, and became a free journeyman of the Merchant Taylors' Company. His wife's name was Elizabeth and they had three children, Edmund (the poet), Elizabeth and John. Edmund himself states in the *Prothalamion* that he was born in London, but that his principal family connections are provincial:

> To mery London, my most kyndly Nurse,
> That to me gaue this Lifes first natiue sourse:
> Though from another place I take my name,
> An house of auncient fame.

128–31

He is apparently here claiming kinship with the Spensers of Althorpe, Northampton. The head of this branch of the family was Sir John Spenser, and Spenser sings the praises of three of his daughters in *Colin Clovts Come Home Againe* under the names of Phyllis, Charillis and Amaryllis, turning yet another reference to the family into a graceful compliment:

> . . . the sisters three,
> The honor of the noble familie:
> Of which I meanest boast my selfe to be,
> And most that vnto them I am so nie.

536–9

Apart from these few facts almost nothing is known or can be guessed about Spenser's parents or his home and childhood. There is, however, every indication that they were not wealthy, for on going to school, and later when they proceeded to Pembroke Hall, Cambridge, both Edmund and John received some assistance (a gown each while they were at school, and on going to Cambridge the sum of ten shillings apiece) from the estate of Robert Nowell, a member of a wealthy Lancashire family, who had left money for benefactions of this kind.

As Spenser's father was a journeyman of the Merchant Taylors' Company, it was almost inevitable that his sons should attend the Company's new school. Spenser was in fact one of its earliest pupils, for it was only founded in the autumn of 1561.

The school was housed in a mansion, called the Manor of the Rose, which had previously belonged successively to various noble families. The statutes provide for the 'better bringing up of children in good manners and literature, to the number of two hundred and fifty'. Of these, up to one hundred might be 'poore men's sonnes and comying together to be taught (yf suche be meete and apt to learne), without anything to be paid by the parents'. Fifty more might be admitted on the payment by 'their poore parents or other of their friends' of two shillings and two-pence each quarter. The remaining hundred, 'being riche or meane men's sonnes', were to have their full fees of five shillings each quarter, paid by their parents or friends. We do not know to which of these groups Spenser and his brother belonged, but since they benefited from the Nowell estate they were probably not amongst those who paid their fees in full.

The statutes of the school, as laid down at its foundation, are both practical and intelligent. Perhaps the most remarkable thing about them is the way in which the members of the Company have confined their specifications to the ensuring as exactly as possible that the conditions of their school and its running shall be conducive to study and learning, without attempting to implement any particular syllabus, or even to insist on any theory or method of education. About the purpose of the school, and indeed of education as such, they are quite clear: 'for the bringing up of children in good manners and literature'. By which they would mean Latin, and possibly Greek. Not being themselves scholars, they have been imaginative enough to confine themselves to the practicalities necessary to this end. So they are determined to make every possible provision for the welfare of the pupils in every domestic particular, even to the rule that no tallow candles, but only the more expensive wax kind, are to be used. Again, they lay down strict rules for the discipline of the school, ensuring that its aims shall not be vitiated by the idle or rowdy behaviour of the pupils:

> The children shall come to the schoole in the morning at seaven of the clock both winter and somer, and tarry there untill eleaven, and

returne again at one of the clock, and depart at five, and thrice in the day, kneeling on their knees, they shall say the prayers appointed with due tract and pawse, as they may be . . . (that is to say) in the morning, at noone, and at the evening.

At a period when most people's day was governed by the sun, when it was normal to rise at dawn, and leave off work as soon as possible after sunset, the early beginning of the school day would not have been very remarkable. Spenser in all his poetry shows an unusual sensitivity to the changes of light; to the freshening glory of dawn, and the dark glooms of evening: almost always they have on the one hand hopeful, on the other sinister or sorrowful significance. During the winter he must have risen before dawn to get to school, but the bleak and chilly memory does not seem to have affected his imagination in any way! On the other hand, like the majority of his contemporaries, Spenser owes much to the custom of prayers said thrice daily in school. These would for the most part consist of following the Psalms (appointed for every day of the month), as the injunction that they are to be spoken 'with due tract and pawse' indicates. The English version by Coverdale, still found in the Book of Common Prayer, would be used, and their imagery and phrasing became inevitably familiar both to the ear and to the imagination of the scholars. It is almost impossible to underestimate the influence of the Psalms, even more than the rest of the Bible, on the literature of the period. Coverdale's translation of the Psalms is, as a 'background book' alone, quite indispensable.

While they were in school the pupils were not allowed to take food or drink into their classrooms, and the statutes are firm on this matter and on such amusements as might lead to quarrelsome or unruly behaviour:

'Nor lett them use cock-fighting, tennys-play [that is, 'real tennis'] —nor riding about of victoring, nor disputing abroad, which is but foolish babling and losse of time.' 'Disputing' here would probably mean holding academic debates, and the prohibition is interesting. It shows how 'modern' the Company intends the school to be, for the dispute is the medieval method of teaching and of learning. A scholar would state his thesis, and prove it under heads or divisions of his subject, and these his opponent would attempt to refute, on grounds of fact or logic; an adjudicator would decide between them. As a method it can produce magnificent results; St. Thomas Aquinas is its greatest exponent. But in the 16th century, to those interested in education and educational reform, it has all the associations of its worst abuses: hairsplitting arguments in which all thought of arriving at or defining the truth is forgotten in the fantastic intricacies of mere cleverness, with a strong element of showing-off on the part of those involved. But as far as 'waste of time' is concerned, the pupils had very little to waste. Each was allowed one 'absence' a year, except in very special circumstances, and during the week either a Tuesday or a Thursday afternoon was free for 'remedye' (that is, recreation) except when there was a public holiday in the week, when the free afternoon was cancelled.

The Company's Council was composed of sober men, with a rigid and austere view of the conditions most likely to lead to sound learning and discipline. How this framework should be fitted in with scholarly curriculum they do not say. As far as the academic workings of the school are concerned they make only one specification, on the matter of entrance requirements. Candidates must know the catechism in English or Latin, and be able to read and write competently, 'or els lett them be admitted in no wise'.

As far as teaching, and the administration of justice and discipline within the bounds of the rules they have set down are concerned, they delegate their authority completely to a man fitted by his training and talents to devote all his energies to administering it:

> The high maister in Doctrine, learning and teching shall direct all the school . . . a man in body whole, sober, discreet, honest, vertuous and learned, in good and cleane Latine literature, [that is to say, language and rhetoric as well as Latin authors] and also in Greeke, iff such may be gotten. A wedded man, a single man, or a priest that hath not benefice with cure, office nor service, that may lett [hinder] his dew business in the school.

The man they chose for this position was magnificently suited to such responsibility. Richard Mulcaster is one of the great educational thinkers of his own, indeed of any age. He was conscientious to the last degree, but of a most original mind and great learning. The Company could have nowhere found a man more capable of making use of the freedom of opportunity they offered him to establish within a few years a tradition whose benefits he might still recognise today.

RICHARD MULCASTER (c. 1530–1611)

Mulcaster was himself educated at Eton, and at King's College, Cambridge. He was a 'Student'—that is, a teacher—at Christ Church, Oxford, from 1555 to 1561, when he was chosen to be the first Head Master of the Merchant Taylors' School. He remained there for twenty-five years, in spite of various disagreements with the governors, on whom he was inclined to look down, as not being men of sufficient learning to appreciate his aims and efforts. He held various ecclesiastical appointments— as Vicar of Cranbrook in Kent, Prebendary of Gatesbury, and Rector of Stanford Rivers. Ten years after leaving the Merchant Taylors, he was elected to the Headmastership of St. Paul's School where he remained until 1608.

Mulcaster was that rare combination: a practical idealist. He was an educational theorist as well as a teacher, and the Merchant Taylors' School gave him the fullest scope for putting his ideas into practice. His two books on education were printed in 1581 and 1582. The first, *Positions*, was concerned with grammar school education and with the whole range of educational problems in society. The second, the *Elementarie*, deals with the education of younger children.

He always sees education as a whole. In the dedication to *Positions* he says:

> I have entitled the book Positions, by cause entending to go on further, for the advancement of learning I thought it good at the first to put down certaine groundes needfull for my purpose, for they that be the common circumstances, that belong to teaching and are to be resolved on, ere we begin to teach.

He is one of the first writers to advocate universal education. Education, in his opinion, should be available to all, according to the capabilities of the individual and the position his talents may fit him to occupy: 'First consider the end, wherefore they are to serve, when they are once learned, and then their qualities, whereby they are to be proved fit for their learning.' Not every child is fitted for the kind of education Mulcaster's own school aims to give, or for the further discipline of the universities. For those who receive such education, it is above all a training for the responsibilities their talents fit them to bear in the commonweal. This is the prevailing attitude of the time: it is echoed by many writers, by Bacon, for example, in his *Advancement of Learning*, but Mulcaster goes further, by what seems to us a natural corollary but which was at the time a revolutionary step. This is his use of English, of his native language, as a vehicle for education and as a subject worthy of study in itself. He says of his own writings: 'I do write in my natural English tongue, by cause though I make the learned my iudges, which understand Latin, yet I mean good to the unlearned, which understand but English. . . . I will serve my country that waie, which I do surely think will prove most intelligible unto her.' His feeling for English was itself a manifestation of patriotism that did not prevent his appreciating the excellencies of foreign lands: 'I love Rome, but London better, I favour Italy, but England more, I honour Latin, but worship English.' He sees classical learning, and the study of foreign literature, not only as ends in themselves, but as the means of enriching his own language, both as to vocabulary and rhetoric. Spenser's work shows the influence of Mulcaster's teaching, especially in his feeling for language.

Mulcaster cites three classical authors in particular to support his views on education: Plato, Aristotle and Quintilian. He does not see any point in the medieval method of heaping up impressive authorities 'which be nothing needful, in such cases as be nothing doubtful'. The same directness of approach applied in his teaching practice. The authors taught were chosen for the excellence of their subject matter and their style; Ovid for his delicacy and elegance of expression, Cicero for his style and weight of utterance, or Virgil as the greatest exponent of epic and patriotic writing. The method of translation and composition and of learning by heart examples of various rhetorical terms and elegant phrases was in some ways arduous, but for Spenser it seems to have preserved the freshness and delight of discovery in what was learnt. In the Prologue to Book VI of *The Faerie Queene*, Spenser addresses the Muses:

> Such secret comfort, and such heauenly pleasures,
> Ye sacred imps, that on *Parnasso* dwell,
> And there the keeping haue of learnings threasures,
> Which doe all worldly riches farre excell,
> Into the mindes of mortall men doe well,
> And goodly fury into them infuse;

(Imps here means 'offspring'—of Apollo in this case.) These lines epitomise beautifully the delight of learning, and of reading, and the sense that poetic creation is always a living continuation; an organic yet independent response.

But Mulcaster's idea of what constituted education was not confined to 'authors', to language and literature. He laid great emphasis on physical training and fitness, and to this perhaps Spenser owes his unfailing delight in open-air recreation of all kinds. Mulcaster was also much interested in music; his pupils had daily practice, both in singing and playing, and the technical part of this training has left its rich mark on Spenser's versification as on his language and imagery. He believed too that acting was a good means of encouraging self-confidence, grace of speech and deportment: 'good behaviour and audacity', as he said, and to this end he presented plays each year before the Court. It is more than probable that Spenser first appeared before the Queen in one or more of these, and his magnificent sense of spectacle, his ability to present scenes and pageants to the mind's eye, may owe something to this early experience. In fact Mulcaster's object was to develop all the talents of his pupils. In this he was in agreement with the opinion of his age, with its high ideal of the 'complete man', whose excellence would show itself in every field of activity. He said: 'It is not a mind, not a body that we have to educate, but a man, and we cannot divide them.'

Spenser was at Pembroke Hall, Cambridge, from 1569 until 1576. He entered as a Sizar; that is, he was required to perform various menial and domestic services in return for which he received free upkeep. Even so, it was probably only the Nowell bequest that enabled him and his brother John to go to university.

Here he made full use of his opportunities to build on the firm foundations of learning already laid. Cambridge was at this time the centre of progressive Humanism. The old, medieval curriculum—of the *Trivium* (grammar, logic and rhetoric) leading to the degree of Bachelor, and the *Quadrivium* (music, arithmetic, geometry and astronomy) leading to the Master's degree —had been largely recast. (Both Oxford and Cambridge still grant their M.A., which also confers senior membership of the university, after twenty terms have passed since matriculation. This is now a formality only, but the 'viva' which often takes place as part of the B.A. final examination has one of its origins in the candidate's public defence of his thesis for the senior M.A. degree.) The course that Spenser followed included mathematics, dialectics or the art of argument, perspective, astronomy and Greek. Spenser was well grounded in Greek, and certainly his contemporaries came to recognise him as a Greek scholar. Ludovick Bryskett, whom he succeeded in 1589 as Clerk of the Council of Munster, writes of him, in a passage that will be referred to again later, as 'not only perfect in the Greek tongue, but also very well read in philosophie, both morall and naturall'.

It is certain that he began to be 'well read in philosophie' at Cambridge, and that he was deeply affected by the most far-reaching change that had come over the university, as a result of its response to Peter Ramus's famous attack on Aristotelian logic in his Paris thesis for the degree of Master. To Ramus, the Aristotelian method had typified all that was most arid and sterile in the medieval tradition of scholarship. He advocated that for the formal mechanics of Aristotle's method, as it had been developed from the 13th century, there be substituted the 'natural light of reason' by the dialectic method exemplified by the

dialogues of Plato. Naturally, the response to this did not stop
short at method: Platonism itself was studied with revived interest
that took in contemporary philosophical writing influenced by it,
especially the Italian Neoplatonists. Spenser's work and thought
were affected by this movement.

The indirect influence of Platonic dialectics appears in every
passage of argument in his poetry. For example, the Prologue to
Book II of *The Faerie Queene* contains a beautiful illustration of
the 'Socratic' question; a question so angled as to arrive at a
proof which is clinched by the inevitable assent of the hearer
(inevitable that is by the light of natural reason!). He is speaking
of Faerie Land, anticipating the criticism that he cannot say
where it is, and adducing by comparison the lands of the New
World that have been but lately discovered:

> Yet all these were, when no man did them know;
> Yet haue from wisest ages hidden beene:
> And later times things more vnknowne shall show.
> Why then should witlesse man so much misweene
> That nothing is, but that which he hath seene?

That his interest in the other subjects of his course was far
from superficial also appears in his writings. Some examples may
serve to show at once the nature of his personal interest and
something of the meaning of 'naturall philosophy' in the period.

Spenser's knowledge of astronomy is put to wide poetic use in
his work. It is based, as one would expect, on the Ptolemaic
system, with the Earth at the centre, and the Sun, Moon, planets
and fixed stars moving round it in concentric spheres. To Spenser
such knowledge, in all its details, is at once a basis and an argument for metaphysical exploration of the state of the world and
of its meaning. The planetary spheres, in the *Mutabilitie Cantos*,
the last part of *The Faerie Queene* as we have it, form not merely a
convenient imaginative setting: they are the actual matter of the
whole debate on change and corruption, its range and meaning,
as will appear when the *Cantos* are discussed more fully. Again,
Spenser uses his knowledge of the effect of the precession of the
equinoxes, which has altered the heavenly positions of the signs

of the Zodiac since classical times, to prove his belief that the whole universe is in a state of gradual decay:

> . . . for the heauens reuolution
> Is wandred farre from where it first was pight,
> And so doe make contrarie constitution
> Of all this lower world, toward his dissolution.
>
> For who so list into the heauens looke,
> And search the courses of the rowling spheares,
> Shall find that from the point, where they first tooke
> Their setting forth, in these few thousand yeares
> They all are wandred much; that plaine appeares.
> For that same golden fleecy Ram, which bore
> *Phrixus* and *Helle* from their stepdames feares,
> Hath now forgot, where he was plast of yore,
> And shouldred hath the Bull, which fayre *Europa* bore.

FAERIE QUEENE V, Prol. 4, 5

The Ram and the Bull are the signs of Aries and Taurus, and Spenser uses the classical legends attached to them as embellishment, as would seem to him appropriate, for poetry could make fitting use of every kind of knowledge in a way that a scientific treatise could not.

The remaining subject on Spenser's Cambridge syllabus was perspective. This may seem to us rather odd, as part of a course not specialising in the fine arts, but that is because the word is now used chiefly to denote part of the technique of drawing. From what was known of the writings of Pythagoras, as well as the other writers of the classical period, including Plato, the theory of harmonious proportion in the structure of the universe was elaborated, in terms as much philosophical as mathematical. Spenser's studies in perspective were the basis, for example, of the 'arithmetical stanza' discussed on p. 17. And certainly he would have read works on the practical, artistic application of the theory, of which many were written during the Renaissance, in England as well as in Italy. It may be of interest to quote from two of the most famous of these, of which Spenser would almost certainly have heard. Leon Baptista Alberti (1404?–72), a brilliant and versatile man, says in his work on painting:

My rudiments, which explain the perfected self-contained art of painting, will be easily understood by a geometrician, but one who is ignorant of geometry will understand neither these nor any other method of painting. So I maintain that a painter has to undertake geometry.

He applies the same method to architecture. Again, Piero della Francesca (1410–92), in his treatise on *The Perspective of Painting* says '... since the mind is incapable alone to judge [the measurement of distant objects], that is, how large the nearer one, and how large the more distant one ... I say that perspective is necessary: because as a true science it distinguishes degrees of size by showing the foreshortening and enlarging of every dimension by means of lines'. (Incidentally George Tharratt, writing in 1944, discusses in some detail how the principles first analysed by such writers as Alberti and Piero are now being directly used and developed in the field of aircraft production drawing: *A Documentary History of Art*, ed. Holt, Vol. I, p. 256.) When Scudamour sees the glory of Venus' temple, his admiration is intelligent, as when he sees:

> ... a bridge ybuilt in goodly wize,
> With curious Corbes and pendants grauen faire,
> And arched all with porches, did arize
> On stately pillours, fram'd after the Doricke guize.

FAERIE QUEEN IV, 10, 6

and such a comment as this, on Medina's castle, is made with full technical awareness:

> It was an auncient worke of antique fame,
> And wondrous strong by nature, and by skilfull frame.

FAERIE QUEENE II, 2, 12

What was probably Spenser's first publication appeared in 1569, the year he went up to Cambridge. It consisted of translations from Marot's version of one of the *Canzoni* of Petrarch, and from some sonnets by Du Bellay which were afterwards included, some of them in an altered form, in his volume of

Complaints published in 1591. They appeared in John van der Noodt's *A Theatre, wherein be represented as wel the miseries and calamities that follow the voluptuous Worldlings As also the great joyes and plesures which the faithful do enjoy. An Argument both profitable and delectable to all that sincerely loue the word of God.* Spenser's contributions are interesting in many ways; they cast light on the development of several of his interests and methods, as will be shown later. In the context of his time at Cambridge they are specially significant in two ways. First, they indicate that his poetic ambitions are present at the time of his going up, and this is interesting, as confirming what we can otherwise judge of his reading, which must have been conditioned by this; his favourite classical author seems to have been Virgil, rather than the more generally popular Ovid. Virgil, as the greatest of epic writers, would be the obvious model for an aspiring writer on the highest themes, and this would indicate an early determination to write on the grandest scale. More particularly, the *Theatre*, as the wording of its title suggests, was a strongly Protestant work, even Puritan in its slant. If Spenser, at the time of his going to Cambridge, was already inclined to the Protestant party of the English Church, then Pembroke Hall must have been at once congenial and disturbing.

CAMBRIDGE AND SPENSER'S PURITANISM

Cambridge had been the great centre of Evangelical reform in England from the beginning of the Reformation, and Pembroke Hall had been conspicuous since about 1530 as one of the colleges most actively interested in ecclesiastical reform. Four years before Spenser went up, the Master of Pembroke Hall, Matthew Hutton, had been one of the five Heads of Colleges who combined to present a memorial to the Chancellor, Cecil, petitioning against Elizabeth's proclamation 'enjoining the wearing of ecclesiastical habits', since many pious and learned men, in their consciences, could not accept such garments as lawful. The resulting storm of controversy on the Church Vestment issue lasted for several years: the seven years of Spenser's residence—1569–76—coincided with its most heated period. In particular the

Admonition to the Parliament, presented in 1571, and attacking the Church of England, proving in twenty-three chapters that its organisation and ceremonials were unscriptural and untenable, was widely read and ran into four editions. Whitgift replied in the next year with his *Answer to the Admonition.*

As far as is known, Spenser took no active part in the controversy, but the constant debate and discussion no doubt helped towards the definition of his own views. It may be as well to outline these here, as far as they can be deduced from his work.

Spenser has often been called a Puritan. Certainly he inclined to the strongly Protestant party of the Church of England, but he was not an extremist; in fact the iconoclastic fervour of the extremist party was abhorrent to him. His description of the activities of the Blatant Beast, which represents destructive slander, shows this. Calidore, the knight who exemplifies the Virtue of Courtesy and whose quest is to restrain the Beast, finds him despoiling a monastery:

> Into their cloysters now he broken had,
> Through which the Monckes he chaced here and there,
> And them pursu'd into their dortours sad,
> And searched all their cels and secrets neare;
> In which what filth and ordure did appeare,
> Were yrkesome to report; yet that foule Beast
> Nought sparing them, the more did tosse and teare,
> And ransacke all their dennes from most to least,
> Regarding nought religion, nor their holy heast.

FAERIE QUEENE VI, 12, 24

Spenser here is far from favouring the Religious Orders, or the abuses of religion associated with them by men of the Reformed Church in England. He speaks of 'filth and ordure', but to tell of this he says is 'yrkesome'. He sees in such actions, on the one hand the base triumph of the mean and stupid at any scandalous and unlovely discovery, and on the other, the subtle evil of making such triumph the excuse for irreverent behaviour. His attitude towards ecclesiastical reform is directed against outward signs not on their own account, but because of the unsoundness of the inward fact. Two examples will serve to show this clearly.

Archimago appears, as Hypocrisie, ready to entrap and deceive the Redcrosse Knight. He dwells in a hermitage, and takes his deceitful mask from the appurtenances of the Roman faith:

> For that old man of pleasing wordes had store,
> And well could file his tongue as smooth as glas;
> He told of Saintes and Popes, and euermore
> He strowed an *Aue-Mary* after and before.

FAERIE QUEENE I, 1, 35

Here Spenser uses the outward forms of Roman clericalism to express the treachery and evil which to him is intrinsic to the Roman faith. In the House of Holiness, however, Spenser is ready to use the traditional imagery to express the essential nature of the truly Christian life. So the spiritual discipline of the Redcrosse Knight is described thus:

> In ashes and sackcloth he did array
> His daintie corse, proud humors to abate,
> And dieted with fasting euery day,
> The swelling of his wounds to mitigate,
> And made him pray both earely and eke late . . .

FAERIE QUEENE I, 10, 26

Later Mercie takes charge of him:

> Eftsoones vnto an holy Hospitall,
> That was fore by the way, she did him bring,
> In which seuen Bead-men that had vowed all
> Their life to seruice of high heauens king
> Did spend their dayes in doing godly thing . . .

FAERIE QUEENE I, 10, 36

Spenser's deep distrust of the forms and ceremonies associated with Rome on the one hand and with the High Church party on the other, in the vestments controversy particularly, arises out of their abuse, as a cover for political and spiritual treachery, or as a slothful and deceitful substitute for true religious zeal. The Fox, which in the *May Eclogue* stands for the Church of Rome particularly, tempts the foolish Kid to destruction by disguising itself as a pedlar:

37

> Bearing a trusse of tryfles at hys backe,
> As bells, and babes, and glasses in hys packe.

239–40

The bells are those rung during the Roman Mass, the 'babes' (dolls) are idolatrous statues, and the glasses tempt to vanity. One of these last:

> . . . out . . . he tooke:
> Wherein while kiddie vnwares did looke,
> He was so enamored with the newell,
> That nought he deemed deare for the iewell.

274–7

and so he is devoured; the price paid is his soul.

But to Spenser it is clear that Reformation consists of far more than the clearing away of empty forms. Where the ministers are not moved by true religious duty, the Reformed Church is in a worse state than before. In *Mother Hvbberds Tale*, the greedy and cunning Ape and Fox meet with a priest who exemplifies this pitilessly. He urges the rogues to enter the Church, and find there an easy life:

> It's now a dayes, ne halfe so streight and sore:
> They whilome vsed duly euerie day
> Their seruice and their holie things to say. . . .
> Now all those needlesse works are laid away:
> Now once a weeke vpon the Sabbath day,
> It is enough to doo our small deuotion,
> And then to follow any merrie motion.

448–50, 455–8

This kind of sanctimonious passivity was in Spenser's eyes as fundamental a misconception of Christianity as the idolatrous deceits of Rome. He must have agreed wholeheartedly with the demand in the *Admonition* of 1571: 'You must displace those ignorant and unable ministers already placed, and in their rooms appoint such as both can and will by God's assistance feed the flock.' This end Spenser sees as only to be achieved by unremitting effort; in particular by preaching, rather than by the lazy reading of Homilies (for the existence of which the negligent priest in *Mother Hvbberds Tale* was grateful).

This constant militant endeavour that Spenser sees as the very action of the life of the Church and the individual Christian life is far from being a denial of what is gracious; rather it provides the fullest earthly opportunity for its exercise. Extremism of attitude is always a loss to Spenser's mind. The ideal is the 'Golden Mean', where everything is in right proportion. So Guyon, the knight whose Virtue is Temperance, comes to the Castle of Medina. Her elder sister, Elissa, with her lover, Huddibras, exemplifies the melancholy sanctimony characteristic of Puritan religiosity:

> She scould, and frownd with froward countenaunce,
> Vnworthy of faire Ladies comely gouernaunce.
>
> FAERIE QUEENE II, 2, 35

The younger sister, Perissa, is the opposite—all worldly frivolity and thoughtlessness:

> In sumptuous tire she ioyd her selfe to prancke,
>
> FAERIE QUEENE II, 2, 36

But Medina, as her name implies, is all that is fair and wise:

> A sober sad, and comely curteous Dame;
> Who rich arayd, and yet in modest guize. . . .
>
> FAERIE QUEENE II, 2, 14

It is this 'mean' that is Spenser's starting point for right religious practice, as for every aspect of the life that should be governed by it.

SPENSER'S LITERARY ACQUAINTANCES: HERVEY AND SIDNEY

During his time at Cambridge, Spenser's closest friend was probably Gabriel Hervey who was elected to a fellowship at Pembroke Hall the year after Spenser went up. He was a scholar, and his progressive views (he was an ardent Puritan on the one hand, and a determined follower of Ramus on the other) put him straightway in the active radical party of the university. He was by temperament irascible and tenacious; his writings exemplify the most violent and in many ways the most unconstructive side of 16th-century controversial method.

His lectures on rhetoric had a great following. Spenser must have attended them, and it seems likely that the foundation of their friendship lay in their passionate interest in the future of English letters, especially poetry. Hervey strongly advocated the 'reform' of English versification, that should deduce a method and rules from the standing examples of classical achievement; and in the correspondence between them—the letters written in 1579–80, after Spenser's leaving Cambridge—discussion on this topic forms one of the main themes. Another is that of patronage. Both Spenser and Hervey speak of their noble acquaintances; Spenser writes: 'As for the two worthy Gentlemen, Master Sidney and Master Dyer, they have me, I thank them, in some use of familiarity. . . .' In the same letter Spenser refers to an audience with the Queen, but gives no particulars: 'Your desire to heare of my late beeing with her Maiestie muste dye in itself.' The letter was written from Leicester House, and it seems likely that he owed his acquaintance with Leicester himself—at that time the Queen's favourite and the most powerful supporter of the extreme Protestant party of the Church—to Sidney. Politically, Spenser was of their party. But the real bond of sympathy between Spenser and Sidney and, on Spenser's side at least, of admiration, was their interest in the future of English letters.

Sidney was in no position to offer much in the way of financial patronage. It is important to understand just what his position was in the literary scene of the day, in order to see why his acquaintanceship, his lightest word of praise, was so highly valued—not only by Spenser (his influence on Spenser in particular shows in all his work)—and why the elegies that appeared at his death almost without exception express a sense of personal and wounding loss that has nothing to do with the expected formalities of public grief.

He combined, in talents, deportment and character, all that was most ideally admired in his age. Physically he was attractive and accomplished; he was noted for his horsemanship, for his skill at arms. He was learned, never pedantic, and he numbered among his friends many European scholars. Even his faults—he was proud and of quick temper—consisted in qualities rather admirable to a Renaissance mind than deplorable; the fiery concomitants of a noble temperament. He had a high sense of responsibility to his sovereign and to the State: all his ideals, his accomplishments, as well as his political actions were geared to this public context. Ophelia's description of Hamlet fits him perfectly:

> The courtier's, soldier's, scholar's, eye, tongue, sword;
> The expectancy and rose of the fair state,
> The glass of fashion and the mould of form,
> The observ'd of all observers . . .   HAMLET III, *1*, 150–3

He was universally admired and praised, in Europe as well as at home. And if he seems, in the retrospect of his heroic death, to be too excellent, too much the ideal but tragic luminary of Elizabeth's court; if we suspect that some of the brightness is reflected from the tragedy, there are two pieces of evidence to the contrary. One is Spenser's portrayal of him as Sir Calidore:

> In whom it seemes, that gentlenesse of spright
> And manners mylde were planted naturall;

> FAERIE QUEENE VI, *1*, 2

The other is his biographer's own epitaph, composed half a lifetime after Sidney's death, when all mere glamour must have faded: 'Fulke Greville, Servant to Queen Elizabeth, Councillor to King James, Friend to Sir Philip Sidney.' Spenser was not the only one to remember his acquaintanceship with Sidney all his life, being constantly influenced by, and glorying in, the memory.

With all else, Sidney was a poet. His sonnet sequence, *Astrophell and Stella*, is perhaps, after those of Shakespeare and Spenser, the greatest of his age. And it was typical of him that this talent, and the great delight, the exquisite and eager appetite for all manner of literature that went with it, should be based on a profound concern for the place and function of poetry in the State.

As has already been pointed out, this period was not as yet one of poetic achievement in England. Moreover, poetry itself, as an art, was the subject of attack by Puritan writers: it was frivolous, it inclined to vice, to adultery; its very delights were fabulous lies

—and had not Plato banished poets from his Republic? A number of poets wrote in the defence of their art. Poetry was inspired: were not the Psalms of David poetry? Did not the Heavenly Spheres move in Harmony? Did not poetry present truth, whether Theological, Philosophical, Historical or even Scientific, in a fitting because a delightful manner?—and so forth. In 1583 Sidney wrote his *Apologie for Poetrie*, which was widely circulated amongst his acquaintances, though not printed until 1595. Here poetry had found a fitting champion: not a professional, but one whose concern arose from his very awareness of his own status, and of the kinship between the responsibilities of the statesman and the writer. His presentation of his arguments has a graceful, modest detachment, at striking variance with the tone of the controversy into which he is entering: 'I will give you a nearer example of my selfe, who (I know not by what mischance) in these my not old yeres and idlest times, having slipt into the title of a poet, am provoked to say something unto you in the defence of that my unelected vocation, which if I handle with more good will than good reason, bear with me. . . .' His strongest arguments are noticeably given the wide, public context. 'Art for art's sake' was no motto of Sidney's—nor Spenser's: 'Nay truly, though I yield that Poesie may not only be abused but that being abused, by the reason of his sweete charming force it can do more hurte than any other Armie of words. . . . With a sword thou maist kill thy Father, and with a sword thou maist defende thy Prince and Country.'

That Sidney and Spenser would be in agreement over the status and function of poetry is clear. And this mutual interest and concern went farther than mere ideals. Like Spenser at this period, like Hervey, Sidney was concerned with the technique of poetry: with the desirability of reliable critical standards from which poets might work to establish and glorify English. Sidney, Dyer, Fulke Greville and others, with Sidney's sister, the charming and talented Countess of Pembroke to whom he dedicated his *Arcadia*, formed a circle, to which it would seem Spenser had the entrée. They wrote, they read, they talked; no doubt as young, enthusiastic and gifted people will do. And it seems as if they had some plan of forming a society, the Areopagus, that should perform in England the same function as the Pléiade in France: consciously refining and establishing standards for the literature of their time. Spenser himself writes of this: 'And now they have proclaimed . . . a generall surceasing and silence of balde rymers and also of the verie beste to: insteade whereof, they have by an authoritie of their whole senate, prescribed certaine Lawes and rules of quantities of English sillables for English verse: having had thereof already great practise and drawen mee to their faction.'

Hervey himself had the strongest possible views on the subject of reformed versification, advocating that it be based on the metrics of classical poetry. This was logical; the greatest examples should provide the surest models. But Latin verse—Greek too—bases its scansion on the length of syllables, whereas English is a heavily accentuated language, and falls naturally into accentual patterns. An example of Hervey's poetic endeavours in this direction will serve at once to illustrate and condemn the approach. Here he is attempting to write English hexameters: I have scanned one line as an example.

What might I call this Tree? *A Laurell?*

O bonny Laurell:

Needes to thy|bowes will I|bow this|knee, and

vayle my bon|etto.

Who but thou, the renowne of Prince, and

Princely *Poeta?*

Th'one for Crowne, for Garland th'other

thanketh *Apollo.*   ECOMIUM LAURI 1–5

Nor are Spenser's attempts much better. This was a dead end, though one that writers and critical theorists to the end of the century were unwilling to let die. (Indeed similar attempts, more and less serious, have been made in all subsequent periods.) Spenser abandoned it almost at once. We do not know how

43

seriously he struggled with it. His *Epithalamion Thamesis*, in particular, perhaps also his *Dreames*, his *Dying Pellicane* (none of which survive in their original form) may have been written in this vein. But *The Shepheardes Calender*, his first original published work, was not. Rather he went for his models to earlier English writers, especially Chaucer. Nor was *The Faerie Queene*. Hervey's comment on the first three Books, evidently sent to him in manuscript, must be seen as revealing the hurt disappointment of an opinionated scholar whose pupil flouts in practice the methods and, it would seem to Hervey, the examples most dear to him:

> In good faith I had once againe nigh forgotten your *Faerie Queene*: how beit, by good chaunce, I have nowe sent hir home at the laste, neither in better nor worse case than I found hir. . . . If so be the *Fairye Queene* be fairer in your eie than the *Nine Muses*, and *Hobgoblin* runne away with the Garland from *Apollo*: Marke what I saye, and yet I will not say that I thought; but there an End for this once, and fare you well, till God or some good Aungell putte you in a better minde.

It says much for Hervey, who was not good at forgiving or at changing his opinions, that he did retract in this instance, and wrote a dedicatory sonnet which appeared with the published version of Books I–III.

Spenser's associates at this time were then the most progressive, the most accomplished and the most renowned of the writers and noble *literati* of his day. From the point of view of intellectual companionship, of stimulus, of mutual delight, he was well placed. But not even poets can live by inspiration alone.

SPENSER'S CAREER

Spenser complains in the *October Eclogue*:

> But ah *Mecænas* is yclad in claye,
> And great *Augustus* long ygoe is dead: 61–2

In the 16th century a gentleman could not make a profession of letters: above all not of poetry. It was possible to be a playwright like Shakespeare, or a pamphleteer like Nashe, and by this means to make a livelihood, but neither activity was held in the highest literary regard. The aim of such writers was first and foremost to appeal to a widely ranging audience, and this alone, all other considerations apart, would, in the critical and even the philosophical opinion of the time, vitiate the purpose of their work in the highest sense. This purpose is indicated clearly in Spenser's *Letter to Raleigh* 'expounding his whole intention' in *The Faerie Queene*: 'The general end therefore of all the booke is to fashion a gentleman or noble person in vertuous and gentle discipline.' This more or less sums up the argument put forward by Sidney and others in 'defence' of poetry, as a definition of its highest function and true aim. Two possibilities were open to a writer who, like Spenser, viewed his work and his talents in this way. He might find a patron, noble and like-minded, a Maecenas or Augustus to his Virgil, who would supply him with the means to pursue his vocation unhindered by monetary considerations, or he might be helped to a position which carried with it sufficient money to live on.

It seems unlikely that Spenser ever had any real hope of a patron of this kind, though his acquaintanceship with Leicester evidently gave him his highest hopes of a lucrative opening. From the letter he wrote to Hervey in October 1579, we gather that Leicester is thinking of employing him; he talks of being about to take a journey 'to his Honour's service'. But these vague hopes are tempered by a certain realism. He says: 'Whiles the iron is hote, it is good striking; and the minds of Nobles varie as their Estates.' And it seems nothing came of it. All we know is that the following year, 1580, Spenser departed for Ireland as secretary to Lord Grey.

This was not his first visit to Ireland. In July 1577 it would seem from a passage in his *Veue of the Present State of Ireland* that he was in Limerick, and there witnessed the execution of Murrough O'Brien. He was probably there either as secretary to Lord Henry Sidney, father of Sir Philip, and then Lord Deputy in Ireland, or as a bearer to him of dispatches from Leicester. This is a good indication of the kind of position in which he found himself. His friends and influence were such that temporary, almost casual, posts were fairly readily available. So in the following year,

1578, we know that he was acting secretary to Dr. John Young, who, after being first Chaplain to the Bishop of London, then an examiner of Spenser's old school and later the Master of Pembroke while Spenser was actually a student there, had by this date become Bishop of Rochester. He was therefore in a position to offer help and influence of the same kind, but in a totally different sphere, as Spenser's courtly acquaintances.

There is no evidence that Spenser ever considered an ecclesiastical career, however, nor that he desired a university post, to both of which Young could no doubt have helped him. He centred his hopes of an established position on the Court, for two probable reasons. His acquaintanceship with Sidney, and so with Leicester, was more than a mutual sympathy of ideals, literary or political. In Sidney especially was exemplified for Spenser a living ideal of noble activity. The Court, the dynamic centre of the State, provided the fullest focus of idealism; the proper sphere for the poet's function as Spenser conceived of it. This appears quite explicitly in the portrait of the true Courtier in *Mother Hvbberds Tale* (713–92) for which Sidney was the exemplar. The Courtier is contrasted with the general run of courtly parasites:

> For though the vulgar yeeld an open eare,
> And common Courtiers loue to gybe and fleare
> At euerie thing, which they heare spoken ill,
> And the best speaches with ill meaning spill;
> Yet the braue Courtier, in whose beauteous thought
> Regard of honour harbours more than ought,
> Doth loath such base condition, . . .

He is no deceiver, nor a flatterer; he is a man of action:

> Of knightly feates, he daylie doth deuise;
> Now menaging the mouthes of stubborne steedes,
> Now practising the proofe of warlike deedes,

He is a poet, and therefore, naturally, a true lover, and he delights in music, and in letters and learning:

> With which he kindleth his ambitious sprights
> To like desire and praise of noble fame,

> The onely vpshot whereto he doth ayme:
> For all his minde on honour fixed is,
> To which he leuels all his purposis,

This honour does not, however, end in the sterility of self-satisfaction:

> And in his Princes seruice spends his dayes,
> Not so much for to gaine, or for to raise
> Himselfe to high degree, as for his grace,
> And in his liking to winne worthie place;

His talents are versatile:

> For he is fit to vse in all assayes,
> Whether for Armes and warlike amenaunce,
> Or else for wise and ciuill gouernaunce.

In his every action, his virtue is more than an adornment to the Court and his sovereign. It acts dynamically, raising, refining, and glorifying his sphere of action with the man himself:

> Of all the which he gathereth, what is fit
> T'enrich the storehouse of his powerfull wit,
> Which through wise speaches, and graue conference
> He daylie eekes, and brings to excellence.

It is clear from the dedication to *The Faerie Queene* (p. 21) that Spenser sees his poetic function as in every way the complement and corollary of this, when he 'consecrates' his labours to 'live with the eternitie' of his sovereign's fame.

It was natural then that Spenser should turn to the Court, and to such influence as he had there, in his quest for a position from which he might work to this end. But his experience was bitterly frustrating, as is shown in the lines from *Mother Hvbberds Tale* quoted on page 20.

In 1579 he had published *The Shepheardes Calender*, and a number of his other works had circulated in manuscript among his friends. These included probably the *Hymnes to Love and Beautie*, and a part of *The Faerie Queene*. He had in fact made his mark, and gained some reputation as a poet and as the sort of poet he felt himself called to be. It would seem from Spenser's dedication 'To the Earl of Leicester, late deceased', in the preface to *Virgils Gnat*, not published until 1591, that during this period he offended Leicester, and lost his fairest hopes. When he obtained preferment as secretary to Grey, the new Lord Deputy of Ireland, it was not what he had most wanted, though it was a good position in itself; neither did it prove to be what any admirer of Spenser's would have wanted. For Lord Grey, whose policy of ruthless repression in Ireland remains one of the most savage blots on the history of the time, had a great influence on Spenser and on his imagination. The religious intensity with which he carried out his policy, combined with his unpopularity at home and in particular with the Queen, combined to make him appear to Spenser, who shared many of his preconceptions (especially his hatred of Roman Catholicism which Grey saw as the main cause of the revolt in Ireland), as something very like a martyr. From this impression of unflinching duty, Spenser's figure of Artegall, the knight who in *The Faerie Queene* stands for Justice, took shape; and Book V, whose subject is Justice, is, as a result, not merely unsympathetic; it presents an almost heartbreaking perversion of the Virtue with which it deals. Artegall is not so much impartial as ruthless. He does not restrain, much less correct, vice; he eradicates it. In fact, in the Aristotelean terms of Spenser's own age, he is not Justice at all, for Justice should reside as the mean between Indulgence and Severity, and Artegall's fanatical temper is entirely repressive. The full effect and scope of this influence on Spenser's poetry will be better considered in discussing *The Faerie Queene* itself, but this aspect of Spenser's association with Grey needs mentioning here in order to provide a focus for a résumé of his life and activities in Ireland from 1580 onwards.

From the time he arrived in Ireland until about 1588, Spenser lived mostly in or near Dublin. In 1582 he took out a six-year lease on a house in the city, and also leased the New Abbey in County Kildare, where he was Commissioner of Musters in 1583–4.

Dublin was the centre of English administration; Parliament

met in Dublin Castle, which was well fortified, and so sometimes did the Courts of Law. It was the Lord Deputy's official residence, and as his secretary, Spenser would spend much of his time there. Opposite page 89 is reproduced one of the illustrations to John Derricke's *Image of Irelande* showing Sir Henry Sidney leaving the Castle. The heads of traitors, stuck on pikes at the entrance, were a constant feature.

The city was walled, with the sea to the south and open fields to the west. There were many beautiful buildings, and it was by no means lacking in social manners, in wealth and entertainments, and in a strong sense of tradition and antiquity. Spenser would find especially interesting the reports he would have heard of the Pageant of St. George, formerly enacted at the Chapel of St. George. For this a horse was provided by the Mayor, the Elder Master of the Guild was responsible for finding a maiden to lead the dragon, and for dressing her richly, and the Clerk of the Market provided a golden lead for the dragon itself.

There were many men in something like Spenser's position, men of letters who had found employment of various kinds. Among these was Ludovick Bryskett, the introduction to whose *Discourse of Civil Life, Containing the Ethic Part of Moral Philosophy*, was quoted on page 31 for its praise of Spenser's learning. Bryskett, who had preceded Spenser as Clerk of Chancery in 1587 and whom Grey appointed secretary of the Munster Council in 1582, was a close friend of the poet's. Spenser would have known Geoffrey Fenton, too, who also held a secretaryship under Grey, and whose translations from Boisteau and Belleforest, *Certaine Tragicall Discourses*, he had dedicated to the Countess of Pembroke. Barnabe Googe, who had been associated with the first Earl of Essex in his attempts to colonise Ulster, remained in Ireland until 1585; and the possibility of his acquaintanceship with Spenser is particularly interesting, for he was the translator of Marcellus Palingenius' *The Zodiacke of Life*. This work, encyclopaedic in scope and philosophic in treatment, rivalled Mantuan's pastoral poetry in popularity among Renaissance Latin poems. Gabriel Hervey praised it as 'most learned . . . a pregnant introduction into Astronomie, and both [natural and moral] philosophies'. That Spenser had read this work is certain.

Spenser, then, did not suffer from a lack of congenial acquaintances during these years. But his duties can have allowed him little leisure. He would have accompanied Grey on all expeditions of repression against the constant threats of rebellion. Some years later he wrote *A Veue of the Present State of Ireland*, as a carefully reasoned defence of Grey, and the descriptive passages are clearly drawn from direct experience gained then. One of the most famous may be quoted. Besides its own interest, and the implications of tragic unrest and violence that beset Ireland at this period, it serves both as commentary on Grey's policy and on the way political reasoning can deaden all human feeling.

The book is in the form of a dialogue between Eudoxus (Learned) and Irenaeus (Peaceful). Near the beginning Irenaeus has said:

> All lawes are ordaynd for the good of the commonwealth and for repressinge of lycensiousnesse and vyce.

Later, after much discussion and description of the Irish, their habits and customs, unsympathetic as only a conscious representative of a 'superior' people can be to what is both alien and potentially dangerous, Eudoxus asks:

> 'How then do you thinke is the reformaccion thereof to be begone, yf not by lawes and ordynances, [which have been shown to be rendered powerless by the recalcitrance of the Irish people]?' Irenaeus answers: 'Even by the sworde, for all those evills must first be cutt awaye with a stronge hand, before any good can be planted.' He then advises, on the basis of Grey's policy: 'The first thinge must bee to sende over into that Realme such a stronge power of men, as that shall perforce bringe in all that rebellious rout of loose people which eyther doe stand out in open Armes or in wanderinge Companies . . .' [The conclusions of this method] 'I assure me will be verie shorte. . . . Although there should none fall by the sworde, none be slaine by the soldyer, yet . . . they would quicklye consume themselves and devoure one another.' [And as proof he refers to the Munster famine of 1580, when there was] 'such wretchednesse as that any stronge harte would have rewed

the same, out of everie Corner of the woodes and glennes they came crepinge forth upon theire handes, for theire legges could not beare them, they looked like Anatomies of death, they spoke like ghostes crying out of their graves, they did eat of the dead Carrions, happy were they that could find them, yea and one another soone after in so much as the verie Carcases they spared not to scrape out of their graves . . . that in a short space there were none almost left and a most populous and pleentyfull countrye suddenlie lefte voyde of man or beast, yet sure in all that work there perished not many by the sworde, but all by the extremitye of famyne, which they themselves had wrought.'

In its moral implications, the last clause is the most horrifying of all, partly because one cannot simply recoil from it as natural to a more brutal age. It is too familiar, too reminiscent in tone of certain reactions in our own century, to the massed bombing raids on Germany in 1944, for example, or even Hiroshima.

Spenser's hatred (no weaker word will do) for the Irish people is only equalled by his love for Ireland, and in particular for the Irish countryside. Here is his description of Northern Ireland:

. . . yet a most beautiful and sweete Countrie as any is under heauen: seamed through out with manie goodly rivers replenished with all sorts of fishe most aboundantlie: sprinckled with verie manie sweete Ilandes and goodlie lakes lyke little inland seas . . . besydes the soyle ytself most fertile, fitt to yield all kynde of fruit that shal be committed therein to. . . .

In fact, where every prospect pleases, and only man is vile. The point is made explicitly at the end of *The Faerie Queene* in the *Mutabilitie Cantos*. Spenser intersperses the solemn matters of these cantos with a tale of a Faun who offended the Goddess Diana who had hitherto delighted in the Irish woods and hills, but after this:

. . . [She] quite forsooke
All those faire forrests about *Arlo* hid, . . .

Since which, those Woods, and all that goodly Chase,
Doth to this day with Wolues and Thieues abound:
Which too-too true that lands in-dwellers since haue found.

MUTABILITIE *6*, 54–5

When Grey was recalled in disfavour after two years' fruitless attempt to force the rebellious Irish into peaceful submission, Spenser remained in Ireland, where he filled a variety of minor posts as a civil servant. In 1586 he received from the Council of Munster, which was following a policy of 'planting' Munster with such English colonists as might be expected to enrich and civilise the ruined country, the grant of the Manor and the Castle of Kilcolman in the county of Cork. In all it consisted of 3,028 acres, and he had under him six English householders; he was obliged to establish English farmers on his land and, unlike most other holders of these seignories, he had no Irish tenants. At the same time the Council awarded various much larger grants to Sir Walter Raleigh, amounting to some 40,000 acres in all, and these lay for the most part about thirty miles to the south-east of Kilcolman. This coincidence was later to provide an opportunity for Spenser and Raleigh to develop their friendship. Since Spenser resigned his Clerkship in Dublin in 1587, when the lease of his house in the city ran out, we can assume that he then took up residence on his estate.

His residence at Kilcolman was far from untroubled. He became engaged in a protracted series of petty lawsuits with his Anglo-Irish neighbour, Lord Roche, Viscount Fermoy. The countryside, which had never really recovered from the famine of 1580, was in a constantly irritable state of ferment, reaching its climax in the Tyrone rebellion of 1598, the year before Spenser's death. It would not seem a very favourable situation for literary work, but Spenser wrote a great deal during this time. Between 1589–91 he wrote many of the poems in the *Complaints: Daphnaida*, *Astrophel*, and *Colin Clovts Come Home Againe*. This last is dedicated to Sir Walter Raleigh, who visited Spenser in 1589. At this time Raleigh had been displaced in Elizabeth's favour by Essex, and had accordingly left the Court and come to Ireland to look over the estates granted him there. He and Spenser had certainly met each other before from time to time, probably at Court, and also in the course of Grey's campaigns, in which Raleigh had taken some part. Raleigh was, like Sidney, a keen scholar and an accomplished poet; his political views, also like Sidney's and Spenser's, were extreme: he despised Burghley's caution, and was forever urging offensive measures against Spain, particularly in the New World, where he had himself followed the buccaneering example of Drake and Frobisher: and he had also founded the colony of Virginia, 'fruitfullest Virginia' as Spenser called it (*Faerie Queen* II, Prol. 2), named in honour of his sovereign. Unlike Sidney, his pride verged on arrogance, and was the main reason for his frequent unpopularity at Court and elsewhere, and he was violent of temper and wide-ranging in ambition. In *Colin Clovts Come Home Againe*, Spenser calls him Marin, 'The Shepheard Of The Ocean', in reference to his exploits at sea, on which he compliments both him and the Queen with a graceful play on the pastoral convention:

> These be the hills (quoth he) the surges hie
> On which faire *Cynthia* her heards doth feed:

240–1

Cynthia, or Diana, virgin Goddess of the Moon, which controls the tides, is Raleigh's complimentary name for Elizabeth in his own poetry. The voyage referred to is that taken by Spenser and Raleigh together before the end of 1589, when both returned to Elizabeth and the Court. Raleigh's restlessness had probably stirred Spenser's own ambition, and the excitement and interest they shared in literature, and in Spenser's *Faerie Queene* in particular, prompted Spenser to try his fortunes again at Court. Raleigh found himself in favour on his return: he presented Spenser, whom the Queen received graciously. The first three Books of *The Faerie Queene*, with their great dedication, and with seventeen complimentary sonnets in which Spenser commends his work to various great and powerful noble men and women, were entered at the Stationers' Hall (where all printed books had to be registered before publication). With it was published the *Letter to Raleigh*, expounding the whole intention of his work.

Probably Spenser hoped that his poetic fame would gain him preferment in England. His hopes were frustrated: no man who appeared at Court first under Leicester's patronage, then Raleigh's, then later Essex's, could hope to be granted a position of responsibility. The policy of Burghley, who had been Secretary of State since the Queen's accession, was in continual opposition to them all, and it was his policy that Elizabeth accepted. Yet *The Faerie Queene* was immediately successful: among all lovers of literature, in particular the Countess of Pembroke and her circle, Spenser's triumph was all he could have wished. But his only public reward for what was avowedly a work to the honour and glory of the State was a pension of fifty pounds a year. Under the circumstances, perhaps he could hardly have hoped for anything more. But his new experience at Court was such as to intensify his previous bitterness. His volume of *Complaints*, published in 1591, included his recent poems, dedicated to noble friends and to ladies of the Court, in particular *The Rvines of Time*, dedicated to the Countess of Pembroke, 'As intended to the renowning of the race of Dudleys and to the eternizing of the chiefe of them late deceased' (Sir Philip Sidney) and also *Mother Hvbberds Tale*, where the satire against the Court, though not the Queen, and by implication against Burghley, is unmistakable. In *Colin Clovts Come Home Againe* under the *persona* of Colin Clout, he praises various ladies of the Court, and of course the Queen herself, but answers the enquiries of his fellow shepherds as to why he ever left such gracious company:

> Happie indeed (said *Colin*) I him hold,
> That may that blessed presence still enioy,
> Of fortune and of enuy vncomptrold,
> Which still are wont most happie states t'annoy:
> But I by that which little while I prooued:
> Some part of those enormities did see,
> The which in Court continually hooued,
> And followd those which happie seemd to bee.

660–7

Spenser returned to Ireland, then, if the tone of these lines is any indication, at least reconciled to his situation: Colin returned home again, to rural (though not, as we have seen, untroubled) seclusion, to appear again under that name, in Book VI, *10*, of *The Faerie Queene*, in the Valley of the Shepherds, piping to the Graces in their dance. This is not false humility on Spenser's part;

when Sir Calidore comes upon the scene by accident, the vision vanishes. It seems that he had come to see the function of a poet as complementary to the active, courtly life, certainly, but as irreconcileable with it even in artistic terms, and that with this resolution he was content.

In June, 1594, Spenser married Elizabeth Boyle, who lived in Kilcolman. She was related to Sir Richard Boyle, afterwards first Earl of Cork. His twelve months' courtship, and the marriage itself, are the subject of his sonnet sequence, *Amoretti*, and the *Epithalamion*. Since we know very little about Elizabeth Boyle, it may be as well to quote Spenser's description of her, idealised as it is, as she appeared on her wedding day:

> . . . ye would weene
> Some angell she had beene.
> Her long loose yellow locks lyke golden wyre,
> Sprinckled with perle, and perling flowres a tweene,
> Doe lyke a golden mantle her attyre,
> And being crowned with a girland greene,
> Seeme lyke some mayden Queene.

EPITHALAMION 152–8

In the following winter, 1595–6, Spenser was again in London, when the IVth to VIth Books of *The Faerie Queene* were entered at the Stationers' Hall. Spenser now enjoyed the favour of Essex, and his *Prothalamion* for the double marriage of the two daughters of the Earl of Worcester praises Essex as: 'Great *Englands* glory and the Worlds wide wonder,' while remembering that Essex House was formerly Leicester House:

> Where oft I gayned giftes and goodly grace
> Of that great Lord, which therein wont to dwell,
> Whose want too well now feeles my freendles case:

136–40

At this time also he published *Colin Clovts Come Home Againe*, the volume containing the *Amoretti* and *Epithalamion*, and the second editions of various earlier volumes, notably Books I–III of *The Faerie Queene*. He also wrote the *Veue of the Present State of Ireland*. It was entered at the Stationers' Hall in 1598, but not surprisingly, in view of its defence of Grey, whose policy had brought him into grave disfavour, it was not sanctioned for publication. It did not in fact appear until 1633.

In 1579 Spenser was again in Kilcolman. He had resigned his Clerkship to the Council of Munster three years before to Sir Richard Boyle; it is possible that this was a private arrangement made at the time of his marriage. In September 1598, the Queen recommended him to the Sheriff of Cork, as being 'a man endowd with good knowledge and learning, and not unskilful or without experience in the world'. He now had four children, and in 1597 he had made provision for his son Peregrine by purchasing the lands of Renny in south Cork. It seems clear that he had determined to make Ireland his established home. It is at this time that he wrote the *Mutabilitie Cantos*, and in them he sets the scene of Nature's great judgement on Mutabilitie on Arlo Hill near his own estate. This magnificent fragment of a VIIth Book of *The Faerie Queene* (if that is what it is) is all we have of his writings of this time. It is also the last of his poetry to survive, and its theme—the final resolution of change, of decay:

> But stedfast rest of all things firmely stayd
> Vpon the pillours of Eternity,
> That is contrayr to *Mutabilitie:*

MUTABILITIE *8*, 2

—makes this at once ironical and appropriate, for in October 1598, the uneasy peace of the province was finally shattered. Tyrone, who had routed the English forces near Armagh in August, sent an expedition into Munster, and total insurrection followed. Kilcolman was sacked and burned. Spenser and his family escaped to Cork: Ben Jonson's story of his having lost a child in the flames of Kilcolman is unlikely to be true. In December he left Cork for London, having been entrusted by Sir John Norreys, President of the province, with dispatches for the Queen. To these he added a statement of his own, containing 'Certayne points to be considered of in the recovery of the Realme of Ireland'. It is the same in opinion and substance as the *Veue*, though briefer and more immediately topical. He seems to have felt that the disaster was in a profound sense a vindication of

Grey's policy, but he hardly had a chance to urge the government to take action accordingly. Soon after his arrival at Westminster he was taken ill and died on 16th January, 1599.

Bearing in mind that Spenser was in receipt of a pension, and that he was at the time a government representative, Ben Jonson's story of his dying destitute in a garret can be discredited. So perhaps can the story that he 'refused twenty peeces from my Lord of Essex, saying that he was sorrie he had no time to spend them'. If true, it points less to cynical despair than to that courteous gallantry in the face of death which was typical of his age: in the 16th century dying was a thing to be done as gracefully, as memorably, as anything in life.

Certainly Essex defrayed the expenses of his funeral. He was buried in Westminster Abbey, near to Chaucer, to whom he owed so admiring a debt. Many noblemen and poets attended the ceremony, flinging into his grave elegies composed in his honour, and the pens with which they had written them. The Queen ordered that a memorial should be erected, but her order was not in fact carried out. It was not until 1620 that such a memorial was raised, by the wish of Anne, Countess of Dorset.

It was a noble wish on her part; a generous and appropriate gesture. But Spenser's real monument, showing him, his virtues and his faults, to posterity exactly, pitilessly and gloriously, is the subject of the following chapters.

3

Spenser as a Poet

I have now given some idea of Spenser's position among the writers and thinkers of his age; of his own attitudes towards the world in which he lived, and particularly towards himself and his work. I have also outlined some of the most important of the ideas current in his lifetime, about learning and poetry especially, and shown his reactions to them. It is time to look in more detail at the way in which these appear in his work, and to discuss the most important of the literary conventions which he used and the poetic methods and techniques which he developed, as well as the influence of other writers, English and foreign, on his work as a whole.

SPENSER'S USE OF ALLEGORY

For a present-day reader, the greatest difficulty in the way of understanding and enjoying Spenser's poetry is his use of allegory. It is no longer a way of thought or of expression natural to us; so, although I have discussed his use of allegory in various special contexts already, it is as well to look at it as a habit of thought (which for Spenser and his educated contemporaries it certainly was) and as a method of presenting ideas to an audience.

The essence of an allegorical statement, or image, is that it has meaning on more than one level: that is, it has more than one meaning, and these are intentional and recognisable. Of these, one, often the least important, is the *literal* meaning.

When St. Paul, and other Christian writers after him, thought about the life of Christ, they saw it as happening at the centre of human history. Everything that went before was a preparation for this supreme revelation. In a special sense, this applied to

Jewish history as recorded in the Old Testament: the real meaning of the events set down there could now be understood for the first time. One or two examples may be given.

The crossing of the Red Sea by the Israelites was seen as a 'type' of Christ's descent into Hell. In the Roman Catholic Easter Vigil Service the reference is made specifically.

God's promise to Eve that she should bruise the serpent's head is taken to refer to Mary, the second Eve, free from sin, whose Son should destroy the power of 'that old serpent', the Devil in this world. Thus in art, Mary often appears treading on a serpent.

Christ Himself likened His crucifixion to the episode of the Brazen Serpent which Moses raised up to protect the children of Israel from a plague of serpents (Numbers 21): 'Even so shall the Son of Man be lifted up': In Wells Cathedral there is a window showing the Brazen Serpent and Christ crucified in two opposite panels, and in medieval art parallelism between the Old and New Testaments is common. So it was a familiar way of thought, even among the uneducated. These examples belong to what came to be called the 'mystical' level of allegory: that is, they refer to the Incarnation of Christ directly in some way.

There came to be in fact four levels—literal, moral, spiritual and mystical—all of which could be present simultaneously; as, following many commentators, I show in this full example:

> The ox knoweth his owner, and the ass his master's crib: but Israel doth not know, my people doth not consider.
>
> ISAIAH 1, 3

LITERAL: There may well have been an ox in the stable at Bethlehem. And the ass on which Mary had ridden.
MORAL: The dumb beasts recognised their creator, but mankind, for whose salvation He had come, did not.
SPIRITUAL: The ox, in the Judaic Law, was a clean beast (being two-horned, with cloven hooves). It was also a sacrificial animal. Here, therefore, it stands for those of the Jewish people, who were chosen and sanctified by God, who believed in Christ. The ass was an unclean beast of burden. It represents the Gentile world 'burdened with sins' as one writer puts it. This explains why, in

59

pre-renaissance pictures of the Nativity, the ox and ass are almost always in the very centre. They are mankind. It is for their sake that this is happening. Even today in Christmas cards for, example, they are still present: this interpretation of the text is the real reason why.

MYSTICAL: Christ rode upon an ass into Jerusalem, 'meek and lowly.' It therefore recalls Palm Sunday, and His humility in taking on humanity, and in submitting Himself to death. The ox, as a beast of sacrifice, refers to Christ's own sacrifice 'one true perfect and sufficient—for the sins of the whole world'. By His death the 'New Covenant' was instituted, and the need for any other victim superseded.

Spenser writes very often on four levels of meaning, and often with a fifth added: political or topical reference. But it is rare for all these levels to be of equal importance in any context. Usually the moral level is uppermost, and before I discuss this, I will give an example of his using all levels at once.

The 11th canto of Book I of *The Faerie Queene* describes the fight between the Redcrosse Knight and the Dragon, (see the illustration between pp. 88–9), who ravages the Kingdom of Una's parents (Eden). *Literally* this is straight fairy-tale narrative. *Morally* it describes the Christian life as a battle against evil, helped by the sacraments of Baptism (the well into which the Knight falls at the end of the first day and from which he rises refreshed) and the Eucharist (the tree, representing the Cross, whose balm heals his wounds at the end of the second day). *Spiritually*, this is the Church Militant on Earth, battling against the Devil (heresy and error) in defence of the Truth in its care (Una, who watches the battle from a hill top), and preserved by the sacraments entrusted to it. *Mystically*, it is Christ during the three days of His entombment, when He descended to Hell and, as tradition held from the 5th century onward, defeated the Devil on his own ground and released the dead who had hitherto been in his power (including Adam and Eve). To this may be added the *political* level, of the Church and State of England battling against the power and error of the Roman Church. Una here is Queen Elizabeth.

This is a very rich and complex passage and I have not analysed it in detail. But Spenser's method, and his way of looking at the episode of St. George and the Dragon and of presenting it, should be clear enough though, put baldly like this, it must give the impression that understanding Spenser is like doing a crossword puzzle rather rapidly. This is not so. Understanding and enjoying him in such a passage with all its levels is far more a matter of training and habit than of detailed knowledge. Of course, since the whole image of the Dragon-fight is an objective one, expected to be familiar, it helps to be able to pick up hints of particular significance, like the references to Baptism and the Eucharist already mentioned. But the mental poise, so to speak, which the enjoyment of such a passage demands, is not itself difficult of achievement. After a time it becomes habitual.

I said earlier that the moral level is predominant in Spenser. This applies throughout his poetry, but in *The Faerie Queene*, his greatest and most complex work, it is particularly important to remember. The reason is fairly obvious. This is not a theological, or principally a spiritual work. Spenser would not have considered himself qualified either by inclination or training to write either; he was not a divine. Its end is a moral one: 'to fashion a gentleman or noble person in vertuous and gentle discipline.' This does not exclude the higher levels, spiritual and mystical, but they enter to give perspective to the whole context of a Book (as in the great allegories, of which the Dragon-fight is one) or to reveal, as in a vision, the ultimate end of a life lived in the 'vertuous and gentle discipline' exemplified. For Spenser writes always as a Christian. So the Redcrosse Knight, beholding the vision of the Heavenly City, sees even the highest earthly glory, to which his mortal allegiance is rightly given, in proper proportion:

> Till now, said then the knight, I weened well,
> That great *Cleopolis*, where I haue beene,
> In which that fairest *Faerie Queene* doth dwell,
> The fairest Citie was, that might be seene;
> And that bright towre all built of christall cleene,
> *Panthea*, seemd the brightest thing, that was:

> But now by proofe all otherwise I weene;
> For this great Citie that does far surpas,
> And this bright Angels towre quite dims that towre of glas.

FAERIE QUEENE I, *10*, 58

In making the moral allegory the predominant level of this great work, Spenser is working within a long established tradition. This is the appropriate method for instructive writing, particularly if it is on a great and elaborate, indeed an epic, scale. One of the earliest works of this kind, and one of the most influential is a poem called *Psychomachia* (The Battle of the Soul), by Prudentius, who lived in the 4th century. Although short, it is epic in style, and it deals with the war waged in the soul by the Vices and Virtues. These are personified, and given suitable characteristics, in a manner familiar to us in later writers.

Spenser's description of Furor, for example, may be derived from Prudentius:

> And sure he was a man of mickle might,
> Had he had gouernance, it well to guide:
> But when the franticke fit inflamed his spright,
> His force was vaine, and strooke more often wide,
> Then at the aymed marke, which he had eide:
> And oft himselfe he chaunst to hurt vnwares,
> Whilst reason blent through passion, nought descride,
> But as a blindfold Bull at randon fares,
> And where he hits, nought knowes, and whom he hurts, nought
>   cares.

FAERIE QUEENE II, *4*, 7

This kind of allegory, of which Spenser makes considerable use, is completely explicit, and economical. Because the qualities, in this case Virtues and Vices, are isolated, their nature can be portrayed objectively. This is even so when the qualities so personified are parts of a whole state of mind, or character, or mental process as in this passage, describing the 'cure' experienced by the Redcrosse Knight in the House of Holiness:

> And bitter *Penance* with an yron whip,
> Was wont him once to disple euery day:
> And sharpe *Remorse* his hart did pricke and nip,

That drops of bloud thence like a well did play;
And sad *Repentance* vsed to embay
His bodie in salt water smarting sore,
The filthy blots of sinne to wash away.
So in short space they did to health restore
The man that would not liue, but earst lay at deathes dore.

FAERIE QUEENE I, *10*, 27

It would have been possible to convey the same sense by describing the Knight's feelings: 'He suffered agonies of remorse and wept bitterly', but Spenser's interest is not in the Knight as an individual, as a novelist's would be in his hero. His subject in this Book is Holiness. He is interested in the way Holiness is to be obtained in the process of sanctification, and in this passage in what might almost be called the mechanics (psychology is too loaded a word) of repentance. For this purpose, allegory is the clearest, even the simplest, method. There is nothing here that is peculiar to the Knight as an individual. The presentation is applicable to the state of repentance in any man: in Everyman, in fact, as the writers of Morality Plays, using the same allegorical method dramatically, would have it.

By the time that Spenser was using it, this kind of allegorical presentation had developed many of its own conventions, particularly descriptive conventions. An example of this has already been given in Spenser's description of Furor. There are many others. Figures such as Envy, dressed in greenish-yellow and devouring a snake, Charity in yellow robes, Faith in white and holding a book (the Bible), and so on, were instantly recognisable. They could be introduced into masques or pictures and be known at once. This did not necessarily mean that they were stereotyped and dead; merely that the author or artist could be sure of his audience understanding his starting point. The way in which such personifications are used is, of course, the poet's or artist's own. In this respect Spenser is enormously imaginative.

The beliefs and traditions—scientific and otherwise—attaching to the natural world, its laws and inhabitants, also provided an objective basis for allegorical imagery. To make this clear, I shall have to digress and go back to the early centuries of Christian thought, though here I can give only a working summary of the attitudes and approaches involved. The whole subject is of great complexity, not least because some of the greatest minds in human history have contributed to these traditions both by using them and by speculating upon them.

Contrary to much popular thought, the growth of Christianity and the development of theology were accompanied from the earliest times by a profound interest in the natural world. The great classical authorities, Pliny and the rest, who had written of natural history and geography and astronomy and so on, were constantly studied and copied; and, if they were largely unquestioned and little of original importance added to them for a long time, this was mainly due to sheer lack of opportunity: it was not for centuries, not perhaps till the Renaissance, that scholars had facilities comparable to or better than those Pliny had enjoyed in classical Rome.

It was also due, however, to the prevailing attitude towards knowledge of this kind. Just as the Bible was God's revelation of Himself to men, showing His nature and purpose, above all in the Incarnation, so the natural world was His Creation, from which more might be learned about Him. And just as the Bible was directly inspired by God the Holy Ghost, so the world, though fallen and imperfect through Adam's sin, was His work, designed to show truth of a more than factual kind. So the habits of beasts, the 'virtues' of plants and minerals and so forth were interesting and often very useful facts. But the allegorical meaning of these facts was important in a higher sense. To take an example used by Spenser himself: the eagle, as the noblest of birds, was the subject of many legends in serious works on natural history. One of these was that, when it grew old, the eagle would fly up into the sun, until its feathers burned away, when it would fall into the sea or into a spring. From this it would arise in fresh, youthful plumage, with its vigour restored. Now, it is a fact that eagles will sometimes dive from a great height into a lake or river, to seize a fish, and that if the fish is very large, it may be pulled under the water, and have a struggle to free itself: sometimes it may even drown. From observation of such incidents the tradition arises. That it has taken the form it has is due, not to simple-mindedness on the part of those who recorded it, but to the meaning such behaviour was thought to have. The eagle plunging from the sun (the vision of God) into water is seen as an allegory of Baptism, by which the soul is restored to its original perfection, sin (the Old Adam) being cast off. Hence the idea that the bird has restored its youth in literal fact. When the Red-crosse Knight, at the end of the first day's fight with the Dragon, falls into the 'living well', Spenser uses the image of the eagle to describe his recovery at dawn. Una is watching anxiously from the hill, and:

> At last she saw, where he vpstarted braue
> Out of the well, wherein he drenched lay;
> As Eagle fresh out of the Ocean waue,
> Where he hath left his plumes all hoary gray,
> And deckt himselfe with feathers youthly gay,
> Like Eyas hauke vp mounts vnto the skies,
> His newly budded pineons to assay,
> And marueiles at himselfe, still as he flies:
> So new this new-borne knight to battell new did rise.

FAERIE QUEENE I, *11*, 34

From one point of view, at least, it is clear that the 'lesson' to be learnt from the traditional behaviour of the eagle (an eyas is a young eagle) is more vitally important than the factual details of its behaviour simply as a bird of prey. And this applies generally where allegorical truth is deduced from natural fact, more and less accurately observed.

This is perhaps the place to point out that the allegorical interpretations of fact often seem to contradict each other. This can happen in two ways. The first, already illustrated to some extent by the episode of the Dragon-fight (page 60) is when different levels of allegory produce very different meanings.

A different kind of contradiction occurs when the 'quality' or 'virtue' of any creature is such that it can be seen as good or evil according to circumstances. An obvious example is the strength of the lion. In biblical allegory, this mighty and noble beast is often a type of Christ: the Lion of Judah. But again—for it is also fierce and terrible—it can be the Devil: 'Be sober, be vigilant; because your adversary, the Devil, as a roaring lion, walketh about, seeking whom he may devour' (Peter I, 5, 8). Spenser uses the lion both as a type of natural nobility and as a savage beast. A lion protects Una, acting in accordance with its nature whereby, traditionally, it spares the helpless and respects fellow royalty (*Faerie Queene* I, 3, 5). And Wrath, in the procession of the Seven Deadly Sins, rides on a lion 'loth for to be led' (*Faerie Queene* I, 4, 33). The strength of the lion is itself a natural quality. It can be for good or ill. Strength, intelligence (the serpent that seduced Eve is evil, but Christ commanded his followers to be 'wise as serpents'), beauty, which can abuse and deceive or inspire the highest passions; indeed, almost all *qualities* are neutral or, rather, double-edged in this way, and the allegorical method exemplifies this with particular clarity. Those qualities that cannot have an evil manifestation (as Courtesy) or that cannot be good (as Hatred) are Virtues or Vices and in Spenser's hands they are shown very exactly. Allegory is never deceived by false appearances or, in Spenser's case at least, by looseness of thought.

Spenser's powers of description are often highly praised. The more one reads his work the more one realises that this aspect of it is not only because of his great skill with words, or his fine observation and accurate senses. He actually thinks visually. The allegorical method is essentially a concrete method. It formulates clear, well-synthesised images. And here Spenser is working in a tradition—what may be called the 'Emblem-Book' tradition.

The fact that many 'morals' and elaborate personifications were intellectual commonplaces of the time crystallised, in the 16th century particularly, into the form known as the 'emblem'. An emblem (the word originally means a piece of mosaic) is, in essence, a picture, with a text in prose or verse expounding its allegorical meaning. The first emblem books were Italian, but the form soon became popular in England. An example from the first English emblem book (Geffrey Whitney—*A Choice of Emblemes*, 1586) is a vivid illustration, in classical style, showing Envy, *Invidia*, and the accompanying verse does little more than point out characteristic and traditional features. One might recognise her from Spenser's own description, though there is some modification of detail:

> . . . malicious *Enuie* rode,
> Vpon a rauenous wolfe, and still did chaw
> Betweene his cankred teeth a venemous tode,
> That all the poison ran about his chaw;
> But inwardly he chawed his owne maw
> At neighbours wealth, that made him euer sad;
> For death it was, when any good he saw,
> And wept, that cause of weeping none he had,
> But when he heard of harme, he wexed wondrous glad.
>
> FAERIE QUEENE I, 4, 30

Clearly Spenser, as one might expect, found the emblem form imaginatively congenial. His first published work was perhaps of this kind, a series of translations with complementary woodcuts, as Van der Noodt's *Theatre for Worldlings* (1569). The theme of mutability, or rather of transience, is always a major theme in Spenser's work from this, his earliest effort, to the very last lines he ever wrote. The verse, or the picture, retain their meaning independently, but together they form a satisfactory whole. Spenser's poetry is much influenced by the form of the emblem. He will often present a very detailed picture, and then comment upon it in just this way. The portrait of *Enuie* is a good example.

Such a form of presentation is in its very nature allegorical. To Spenser and his readers it was not only a convenient technique; it was a habit of thought as well. That is why he can use it in a narrative framework without breaking the flow of the poem as a whole. Even where he is clearly drawing directly on his own visual experience, not on any particular tradition (such as that of the eagle's renewal of its youth), this habit and this method still apply. So, for example, the enemies that besiege the House of Alma, when they attack Guyon and Arthur, are:

> As when a swarme of Gnats at euentide
> Out of the fennes of Allan do arise,
> Their murmuring small trompets sounden wide,
> Whiles in the aire their clustring army flies,

That as a cloud doth seeme to dim the skies;
Ne man nor beast may rest, or take repast,
For their sharpe wounds, and noyous iniuries,
Till the fierce Northerne wind with blustring blast
Doth blow them quite away, and in the *Ocean* cast.

FAERIE QUEENE II, *9*, 16

This kind of elaborate comparison, an extended simile, is known as a *Virgilian* simile. And this brings us to the matter of literary influence on Spenser's poetry.

SPENSER'S LITERARY MODELS

Spenser's attitude to the great literature of the past, especially classical literature, and to the poets of Italy and France nearer his own time, was strongly conditioned in three ways by his education and by his own poetic ambitions.

First, such authors were models of form and style. The training he received in classical literature at school and later at Cambridge was not only in the language but in the rhetoric of Theocritus, Virgil, Ovid and the rest. He would be encouraged to imitate their verbal techniques as closely as possible in double-translation exercises: that is, translating a passage of verse or prose into English, and then back again. And he would have learnt by heart a wide range of the finest passages of description, dialogue and so forth, so that he was familiar with them not only for their own literary excellence, but as 'examples' upon which to base his own style for comparable effects. Spenser's mastery of such rhetorical forms as the extended simile shows the influence of this study.

Secondly, the great authors were models of *decorum* in the Elizabethan sense. They exemplified the treatment most appropriate for different themes and subjects. So it is not surprising that Spenser shows a great stylistic debt to Virgil in *The Faerie Queene*: Virgil was the greatest of epic poets, and his methods of presenting battle-scenes, and of describing the heroic virtues, would give the best models. For the treatment of love, however, and elegiac lamentation, Ovid among classical authors, and Petrarch, Ronsard and others amongst the moderns, would be drawn upon. A writer who had achieved mastery within a particular *genre* of literature was seen as exemplifying, or even personifying a tradition; later writers would follow this and develop it according to their own talents. To break away from it and start on entirely new ground would have seemed to Spenser's contemporaries not so much original, as petty and impertinent. So Spenser, from the time when he began to write, looked to Virgil, not only as the writer of the *Aeneid*, but as exemplifying in his earlier work the right approach to an epic undertaking. Virgil's first works were in the pastoral tradition (see the discussion of *The Shepheardes Calender* in Chapter 5): the *Eclogues*. He then wrote the *Georgics*, which use pastoral material, but expand from this into wider reference, touching on matters of right government and so forth. Spenser follows this apprenticeship in his own terms. His first published work is *The Shepheardes Calender*, a series of twelve eclogues. Some of these do in fact have political and religious reference, for Spenser, unlike Virgil, exploits the allegorical possibilities of this form. He is consciously following the pattern of 'apprenticeship' laid down in the work of his great model. Pope was to do the same, just as deliberately, writing his *Pastorals* and *Windsor Forest* while he was still hoping to crown his own work with a great epic poem. Milton, too, wrote *L'Allegro* and *Il Penseroso* and then *Lycidas*, which employs the form of the pastoral elegy, to touch on the ecclesiastical and political situation of the country, before approaching his epic masterpiece: *Paradise Lost*.

The third way in which the influence of other poets came to affect Spenser's work is perhaps the most interesting, for it shows a particular kind of pleasure and interest Spenser took in his own reading. Again, this requires a short digression.

The medieval scholars who commented allegorically upon the text of the Bible, and who saw allegorical meaning in the world about them, naturally read classical literature in the same way. Virgil, Ovid and other writers were read, not only for their immediate subject matter, but for the 'higher meaning' this was often thought to represent: Virgil was seen as an unconscious prophet in the pagan world, because his *Fifth Eclogue*, which celebrates the birth of a noble child, was taken as foretelling

Christ's birth. (There are passages in the *Eclogue* very reminiscent of the Messianic prophecies in Isaiah.) And Ovid, whose witty love poetry was, taken literally, hardly edifying from a Christian standpoint, was 'moralised': that is, it became the subject of commentaries pointing a moral allegory. So, for example, the story of Pygmalion (a sculptor, who carved a statue of a girl so beautiful that he fell in love with it, and, having prayed to Venus, was at last rewarded by its coming to life) was interpreted as referring to a rich man who fell in love with a servant; who educated her and gave her all manner of gifts. At last, ennobled by his love, she became his equal, and he married her.

Now Spenser was not born and educated in the medieval period, but in the Renaissance. Such an approach to the classics would have been unthinkable at the Merchant Taylors' School or at Pembroke Hall. But it still had its effect. The method, the habit of thought, had been developed: what was different was the way in which it was applied. On the one hand, Spenser, in lifting a simile or an image from, say, Virgil, is following a great stylistic model. But, whereas the force of Virgil's similes is all in their aptness in a fully literal way, Spenser will usually apply them with added allegorical force. An example will make this clear: Calidore attacks the brigands who have laid waste the Valley of the Shepherds. He is compared to a lion:

> Like as a Lion mongst an heard of dere,
> Disperseth them to catch his choysest pray,
> So did he fly amongst them here and there,
> And all that nere him came, did hew and slay,
> Till he had strowd with bodies all the way;
>
> FAERIE QUEENE VI, *11*, 49

The comparison is obviously apt: the impression of Calidore's overwhelming strength, compared with which the savage brigands are helpless deer, is well visualised. But Spenser has not forgotten that the lion is the noblest of beasts, as Calidore is a noble knight, and it is by virtue of nobility, as well as brute strength, that his power is exercised. The simile is derived from Virgil:

As often a ravenous lion, prowling about the high-built stalls (urged by raging hunger), rejoices if by chance he sees the swift wild goat, or the deer with spreading antlers. He grins savagely: his mane stands up, he fastens on the meat and lies down to devour it, the reeking blood dabbles his fierce mouth.

AENEID X, 722

Virgil applies this comparison to Mezentius wreaking havoc among his helpless opponents. The whole point is the brutality, the savagery of the lion. Spenser would have found a lion unsuitable for such an effect of animal terror and degradation, by reason of the noble associations it had acquired. He would prefer to use a wolf or a tiger in such a context. But in using such a Virgilian reminiscence for his own purposes, he is not so much altering his model, as drawing upon him where it *seems to him* appropriate—within his whole allegorical framework and method.

This framework is not derived from Virgil. Spenser might think about Virgil's poetry allegorically, might apply his own techniques in accordance with his own imagination, but he did not read him allegorically, as had his medieval predecessors. The *Aeneid* was the great example of epic; Aeneas' character and its subject, the founding of Rome and the establishment of government and Empire, make it also a morally instructive work, but its central method was not allegorical, nor would Spenser take it to be such. So he looked elsewhere for a model for the form of his great poem.

He found it principally in the *Orlando Furioso* of Ariosto, though Tasso (whose *Gerusalemme Liberata* owes much to Ariosto and Boiardo who preceded him) supplements this influence. Ariosto's epic is one of the most splendidly enjoyable long poems ever written (an Elizabethan translation by Harington gives a very good idea of the original). It is a maze of adventure, the threads beautifully interwoven, and it moves through its vast complexity of episodes with enormous speed and energy. It is heroic—it is also full of comedy and romance and magical wonder. It was not written as an allegory, but Spenser, in common with many Italian writers of his time, and like Harington,

Ariosto's English translator, understood the poem as having an underlying moral intention. He says in the *Letter to Raleigh* (see page 45):

> . . . I haue followed all the antique Poets historicall, first Homere, who in the Persons of Agamemnon and Vlysses hath ensampled a good gouernour and a vertuous man, the one in his Ilias, the other in his Odysseis: then Virgil, whose like intention was to doe in the person of Aeneas: after him Ariosto comprised them both in his Orlando: and lately Tasso disseuered them againe, and formed both parts in two persons, namely that part which they in Philosophy call Ethice, or vertues of a priuate man, coloured in his Rinaldo: The other named Politice in his Godfredo.

Similarly John Harington says in the preface to his translation of the *Orlando Furioso* (1591):

> Men of greatest learning and highest wit in the ancient times did of purpose conceale these deep mysteries of learning, and as it were cover them with the vaile of fable and verse. . . . For the weaker capacities will feede themselves with the pleasantnes of the historie and sweetnes of the verse, some that have stronger stomaches will as it were take a further taste of the morall sence, a third sort, more high conceited than they, will digest the Allegories: so as indeed it hath been thought by men of verie good judgement, such manner of Poeticall writing was an excellent way to preserve all kinde of learning from that corruption which now it is come to since they left that mysticall writing of verse.

More attention will be paid to Spenser's debts to Boiardo (1434–94), Ariosto (1474–1533) and Tasso (1544–95) in the next chapter. Here I am chiefly concerned with Spenser's reasons for choosing them, and particularly Ariosto, as models.

They were writers, not of the classical period, but of Spenser's own time. That is, their ambition was in some ways very like his own, to write verse equal to that of the greatest known poets, and to write it in their own language, so enriching it. Spenser's reading of the *Orlando Furioso* as a moral allegory would make the similarity of their general aims even greater. Moreover, Ariosto dedicated his work to the House of Este, the rulers of

Ferrara; and just as Spenser makes his Britomart and Artegall not only figures of Chastity and Justice who politically refer to the Queen and to Lord Grey, but also in the actual narrative level of his poem, the ancestors of British royalty and so of Elizabeth, so Ariosto makes Bradamante and Ruggiero, two of his principal characters, the ancestors of the House of Este. As one might expect, Books III–IV of *The Faerie Queene*, where Britomart and Artegall are the central characters, draw most heavily on the *Orlando Furioso*.

Apart from its moral significance, Spenser was clearly attracted by the *form* of the *Orlando Furioso*: its skilful entwining of different narrative threads, and the variations in texture—romantic, heroic and descriptive—for which this method gave opportunity. Indeed, it is the perfect technique for his purpose: it gives every facility for the building up of allegorical structure, and for concentrating on and developing specific levels, as described. *The Faerie Queene* moves much more slowly than the *Orlando Furioso*, part of whose brilliance is in the sheer dexterity of narrative complication. In a way, Spenser is using the same method to achieve an almost opposite end. The four-, sometimes five-level significance of his allegory is drawn out and, as it were, reflected in the structure of his poem.

Although his formal debt to Ariosto is very great, Spenser's imagination is in fact more nearly akin to that of Tasso, whose descriptive writing, as will appear in the next chapter, greatly influenced him. In particular, the whole description of the Bower of Bliss in Book II of *The Faerie Queene* owes a great deal to the gardens of the enchantress Armida in the *Gerusalemme Liberata*.

To return for a moment to the form of *The Faerie Queene* as Spenser must have planned it. Ariosto provided him with a method certainly, and with various episodes. But the kind of epic poem that Spenser wished to write falls into a more complex category.

I have already set out the arguments used, particularly by Sidney, to *defend* poetry against its Puritan detractors in England (p. 42). The *Letter to Raleigh* is itself a defence of this kind. Spenser is anticipating attack both from such conventional classicists as Gabriel Hervey, whose disapproval was quoted on page 44, and from the opponents of poetry in general, particularly poetry using the methods and traditions of romance. He may have been helped in the formulation of his arguments by Geraldo Cinthio, one of the great Italian apologists of romance, who in 1549 wrote his *Discorso intorno al comparre dei Romanzi*. Cinthio distinguishes three types of heroic poem: that which sets forth the action of one man (Aristotle's description of the epic), that showing many actions of many different men (as the *Orlando Innamorato* of Boiardo and Ariosto's *Orlando Furioso*) or a biographical poem such as the *Teseida* of Boccaccio (which was, incidentally, Chaucer's principal source for *The Knight's Tale*). Now, seen as a whole, *The Faerie Queene* can be taken as falling into the first category, since Prince Arthur is the chief character, representing Magnificence, in which all the other Virtues are included, but it falls more obviously into the second. Each Book however, as it deals particularly with the expression and development of a single Virtue, can be seen as falling into the third. The whole shape and structure of *The Faerie Queene* in fact illustrates Spenser's attitude to literary tradition and authority. The models are there to be used. The way they point is open. To follow the established traditions is actually to develop them. Literary tradition as Spenser saw it and made use of it, was an organic, a growing thing.

It is important to see what were the critical concepts to which Spenser reacted, and how he did so. Once this general pattern is made clear, it will appear remarkably consistent, even in minor ways. And it is clear that Spenser considered himself to be in the forefront of the literary practice of his age, since he treats the Italian poets as authorities: he is not a 'pure' classicist (who would end by being a writer of pastiche). But he has a very great respect for literary and critical tradition, classical and otherwise. Hence his deliberate use of archaism and his admiration for Chaucer and other earlier English poets, as well as his use of deliberate and recognisable Virgilian reminiscence. He sees himself as the latest English writer in a tradition; the *whole* European tradition as he recognised it.

Critical theory is deduced from literary practice. As practised by Aristotle and Horace, and by Sidney and Puttenham in Elizabethan England, it consisted in formulating rules by analysing available writing: by isolating its essential elements. Aristotle's definitions of tragedy and epic were not just made, but were derived from analysis of the works of the tragedians and epic poets of his own and preceding generations. So much may seem obvious. What would have seemed equally obvious—to Aristotle, to Plato, to Cinthio, to Spenser, but less so to us—was that literary excellence has a moral as well as an artistic implication. Aristotle bases his literary theory on the assumption that certain moral qualities, good and evil, will be recognised as such, and that certain reactions, as of pity and terror at the fall of a great man, may be counted upon and have in themselves a moral effect. From critical theory to moral philosophy was, then, a very short step; and for Christian writers such as Tasso and Spenser, from moral philosophy to theology was equally so. Spenser's whole plan in *The Faerie Queene* is designed to express the highest truth in the best way: his moral purpose demands this artistic method. This expression is deliberate and conscious; he makes full use of his learning as well as of his belief. His moral concepts, his ideas of 'virtuous and gentle discipline', are formulated and expressed in philosophical terms, both classical and Renaissance.

ARISTOTLE, PLATO AND NEO-PLATONISM: THEIR INFLUENCE ON SPENSER'S POETRY

In this section I can only give a brief outline of Spenser's use of particular philosophical concepts. Most of what I say follows from the details of Spenser's reading and education already described, and the short book list (p. 174) contains suggestions for further specialised reading.

It is first necessary to outline, very briefly, the history of the Aristotelean and Platonic philosophies in Europe.

Plato taught that everything in this world is an imperfect copy of its essential nature. So all roses are copies of the Essential Rose, or to use his own term, of the Idea Rose. As such, they are imperfect: they are less real than the Idea, though the more perfect a particular rose may be, the more nearly it approaches to the perfect Reality, and the more readily it suggests it. So with qualities: a *beautiful* object, or person, or action suggests Beauty itself. And, by loving first a particular beautiful person or thing, a man may come to love all beautiful things; then to see the beauty of character, and of such abstract formulations as law and government; and, finally, come to love and approach Beauty itself, or Perfection.

Aristotle taught that qualities only exist by virtue of their expression. So the concept of what a tree is, or should be, only exists because there are particular trees. The concept of what courage is exists only because it is exemplified in brave actions.

Now it is very clear that these two basic standpoints will lead to very different approaches, as, for example, to the natural world. And it is also clear that the Platonic standpoint, of the diffusion of perfect essence through the creation, is readily adaptable to Christian expression. Until the 12th century, in fact, Christianity used the Platonic standpoint for philosophical purposes, adapting and elaborating it. The whole system of allegory is essentially Platonic; from the lowest level of truth (literal) one may ascend to the highest (mystical)—that is, the truth about God: Truth itself.

The Aristotelean tradition was discontinued in Western Europe from the end of the classical period. It was taken up by Islamic philosophers. Aristotle was taught and studied in the universities of Islam, notably in Moorish Spain. Córdoba, which, in the 10th century was perhaps the greatest university in the world, was particularly a centre of Aristoteleanism: physics, mathematics, medicine as well as moral philosophy. For the Aristotelean method, of logical deduction from given examples, was a practical method. In fact, Aristotle's scientific works provide the basis of the modern scientific approach.

In the 12th century, various of Aristotle's works became again available in Europe, in Latin translations from Arabic versions of the original Greek. And the effect was extraordinary: it is one of the most exciting moments in the history of human thought.

For here was a whole new world—literally a new way of looking at the world, and of knowing it. Aristotelean logic was a new, a thrilling tool. Its possibilities appeared infinite. Perhaps they were. For it should have been possible to find a satisfactory balance, to stand poised between the view of the world as God's creation—and so in its every manifestation revealing Him, which was the essence of the Christian version of the Platonic method—and the view of the world as God's creation, and so important in its own right in every detail. The division may be illustrated. Albert the Great, in the 13th century, wrote, amongst much else, a treatise on the habits and behaviour of animals. Where possible he, like Aristotle, uses his own observation; but he also uses authorities he takes to be reliable and, when faced with contradictions, he uses Aristotelean logic on the basis of what he does know in an attempt to deduce the truth. At one point he discusses the Phoenix, which had long been thought of as typifying the Resurrection. He cites the authorities, Pliny and others, for its description and habits. Then he says: 'But for the rest, it belongs rather to the study of Theology than to that of Natural Science.' He is right, of course. The methods he has available are good for different purposes. But there is here a crack in the concept of knowledge as a whole entity. The Church became worried at the possibilities of heresy it feared were inherent in the new method. It tried to ban Aristotle from the universities, unsuccessfully, but the damage was done. The balance was lost, perhaps for ever. The crack remained—and widened. Today it looks like an abyss. We hear of the Two Cultures.

But Aristoteleanism established itself. It became the accepted method of learning, and of exposition, until the time of Ramus, who rebelled against the arid manifestations of its scholastic decadence (see p. 31) and who favoured the Platonic approach.

The study of Plato and of the Platonic methods of argument, as he encountered these at Cambridge, had, as we have seen, a great influence on Spenser's way of thought and imagination. But Aristotle's moral philosophy gave him a familiar conceptual framework. Evidently in planning his great work he had in mind Aristotle's dictum, restated by Tasso, that an epic should exemplify a particular Virtue, as Aeneas—piety, or Ulysses—prudence. Hence his full plan of twelve knights, each patronising one of the Virtues. Of course he intended that they should do so not merely by example or illustration, but by full allegorical elaboration. For this moral framework Spenser was indebted to Aristotle's *Ethics*. He says in the *Letter to Raleigh*: 'I labour to pourtraict... the image of a braue knight, perfected in the twelue priuate morall vertues, as Aristotle hath deuised.' The combination of all particular Virtues is itself the supreme Virtue of Magnificence, or Magnanimity. As Spenser says: 'In the person of Prince Arthure I sette forth magnificence, ... for that (according to Aristotle and the rest) it is the perfection of all the rest, and conteineth in it them all, therefore in the whole course I mention the deedes of Arthur applyable to that virtue which I write of in that booke. But of the xii other vertues I make xii other knights the patrones, for the more variety of the history.' So that, including Arthur, Spenser treats of thirteen Virtues, though Magnificence is properly illustrated under each of the twelve other heads.

To Aristotle's list of Virtues, Spenser adds Justice, in place of 'the mean concerning Ambition' as being expressed in Holiness (humility) which is not, of course, an Aristotelean Virtue at all, though the *moral* starting point for its representation is 'High-mindedness'—in Christian terms, the desire for God's grace in all things, for the highest good. In fact, here, as elsewhere in the presentation of the Virtues, once established and defined, Spenser's Platonism takes over, as will be shown presently.

It was Aristotle's central doctrine that any good consisted in the mean between two extremes: the Golden Mean. So Justice is the mean between Indulgence and Severity; Temperance between Excess and Abstinence. This obviously conflicts with the Platonic assumption that the Good is an absolute; ultimately an extreme. But this conflict only appears overtly on the spiritual and mystical levels, which Spenser deals with in general in Platonic terms. The concept of the Golden Mean is of great importance in his work. It is a commonplace of the period, most especially in the terms in which it is presented, for example, by the Earl of Surrey:

Whoso gladly halseth the golden mean,
Voide of dangers advisedly hath his home
Not with lothsom muck, as a den unclean,
Nor palace-like, whereat disdayne may glome.

THE GOLDEN MEANE

In Renaissance thought it is essentially a moral doctrine, and as
such Spenser uses it. It chiefly affects his work in two ways.

First, where it is directly applicable to a particular Virtue. So,
while it does not apply directly to a presentation of Holiness or
Chastity (though it may to some of their practical applications as
will be shown in Chapter 4) neither of which can be seen in
terms of a happy medium, it clearly does apply to Temperance,
and should to Justice. Book II of *The Faerie Queene*, whose subject is Temperance, is in fact the most directly Aristotelean of
all, and in Canto 2, in the presentation of Medina and her sisters
(see p. 39), Spenser gives a full allegorical presentation of this
doctrine. In Book V, whose subject is Justice, the balance is upset
by Spenser's own view of this Virtue, particularly in relation to
the historical allegory, as has been indicated in the previous
chapter. Even so, there is an attempt to apply this doctrine.
Significantly, perhaps, the central allegory used for this purpose
does not involve Artegall, the knight representing Justice,
directly. Britomart (Chastity), his betrothed, on her way to
rescue Artegall from the Amazon Queen, Radigund, sleeps in the
Temple of Isis. She dreams that she is sacrificing to the Goddess
when suddenly her garments are transformed into royal adorn-
ments. In the midst of her happiness, the flame on the altar is
blown by a sudden wind, and spreads, so that she is in danger.
Then the image of the crocodile, beneath the feet of the Goddess's
statue, awakes, devours the flames, and threatens to turn on her,
but is beaten back by the Goddess, when he becomes meek and
pays court to her. In the morning the priests interpret the dream:

> ... that same Crocodile doth represent
> The righteous Knight, that is thy faithfull louer,
> Like to *Osyris* in all iust endeuer.
> For that same Crocodile *Osyris* is,
> That vnder *Isis* feete doth sleepe for euer:

79

> To shew that clemence oft in things amis,
> Restraines those sterne behests, and cruell doomes of his.

FAERIE QUEENE V, 7, 22

Spenser's Justice is not itself the mean, until it is tempered by Love and Mercy from without.

This way of demonstrating the Golden Mean of moral virtue must be carefully distinguished from the Platonic, or rather Neo-Platonic, method of showing virtue in a composite pattern, of three parts, of which Spenser also makes great use. The supreme example of this is the dance of the Graces, which is seen by Calidore (Courtesy) on Mount Acidale in the Valley of the Shepherds:

> Those were the Graces, daughters of delight,
> Handmaides of *Venus*, which are wont to haunt
> Vppon this hill, and daunce there day and night:
> Those three to men all gifts of grace do graunt,
> And all, that *Venus* in her selfe doth vaunt,
> Is borrowed of them.

FAERIE QUEENE VI, 10, 15

The Graces are the 'Handmaides of Venus', because they are Chastity, Beauty and Pleasure, which together make up the complete nature of Love. More than this, they are these qualities *in action*. It is through the manifestation of Chastity, Beauty and Pleasure in this world that Venus is revealed to men: Venus, the Desirable Good itself in one aspect is an absolute, an extreme, an Idea, and as such cannot appear in this world, and is static. But nothing in this world is static. The Dance of the Graces, where each virtue passes into each, interlinked, 'in order excellent', reflects this, as well as showing that perfection is a rhythm, a pattern of its independent parts. The Graces form what is called a Platonic Triad.

The renewal of Platonic studies in the Renaissance meant not only that Plato's *Dialogues* were read and taught and his method of argument adopted, but also that Platonic philosophy continued to develop. The most important newly developed concept was that of the Good (God) unfolding in descending degrees which were formulated as Triads, of one of which the Graces came to be the accepted image. With this went the idea of Beauty (or any excellent quality) being itself divine; in a human being, or in the created world, it is a manifestation of divine origin, and to that origin, in spite of decay and death, it must return. This applies to physical beauty, and still more to virtue—'the beauty of the mind'—by which, in Christian terms, the soul is fitted for Heaven. Just as Christ at His Incarnation became man, and took His Manhood into Godhead at the Ascension, so virtue, divine in origin, takes up the virtuous soul with it on its return to its source. Hence such terms as those Spenser uses in many of his Love Sonnets:

> The glorious image of the makers beautie,
> My souerayne saynt, the Idoll of my thought,
>
> AMORETTI LXI

The great centre of Renaissance Neo-Platonism was Florence. Mirandola, Ficino, and others took up this method and developed it. Their influence was very great: Spenser would have been familiar with their work, and with that of their followers in France and elsewhere. Clearly he found these ideas both exciting in themselves and imaginatively stimulating in their expression.

I have already cited the Graces as an established Neo-Platonic image. (Botticelli uses it, for example, in his *Primavera*, which is no mere casual fantasy, but an extremely complex and intellectual allegory expressing the composite nature of Love.) Almost any mythological reference in Spenser has a philosophical meaning of this kind; this is the way he weaves such references into his allegory. Further examples will appear in the next chapter. (The whole subject of Renaissance Neo-Platonism and its relation to the arts is fascinating: the best book on the subject is Edgar Wind's *Pagan Mysteries in the Renaissance*.)

Spenser is writing about the Virtues, and about the Virtues in action, in this world, where nothing is static. They are the elements of right order, but in this world even that order consists in change. The profound concern with transience, with mutability, that shows itself in Spenser's work and in all contemporary thought, may appear at first sight to result from the apparent conflict between the instability of all earthly life and achievement as contrasted with the ideal, heavenly conceptions that may be at times deduced from them. This is not always so.

For Spenser, there are two ways of looking at the world, and the obvious facts of growth, decay and transience. The first is the natural human reaction, of personal grief and even despair:

> So all the world, and all in it I hate,
> Because it changeth euer too and fro,
> And neuer standeth in one certaine state,
> But still vnstedfast round about doth goe,
> Like a Mill wheele, in midst of miserie,
> Driuen with streames of wretchednesse and woe,
> That dying liues, and liuing still does dye.

DAPHNAIDA 428–34

The second is an objective standpoint, that sees change as itself constituting a pattern. So the old shepherd, Thenot, rebukes young Cuddie's short-sighted despair in the *February Eclogue*:

> Lewdly complainest thou laesie ladde,
> Of Winters wracke, for making thee sadde.
> Must not the world wend in his commun course
> From good to badd, and from badde to worse,
> From worse vnto that is worst of all,
> And then returne to his former fall?

9–14

This is an objective view and a moral one: it operates on the moral level. This is a fallen world; decay and misery are part of its very working. But virtue, a right attitude to misfortune and pain, has its own stability, as shown in the words of the exiled Duke in *As You Like It*: 'Sweet are the uses of adversity' (II, *1*, 12).

But the stability of virtue is naturally heavenly stability. As such, in Christian terms, it has an eternal solution:

> *Dido* is gone afore (whose turne shall be the next?)
> There liues shee with the blessed Gods in blisse,
> There drincks she *Nectar* with *Ambrosia* mixt,

And ioyes enioyes, that mortall men doe misse.
The honor now of highest gods she is,
   That whilome was poore shepheards pryde,
   While here on earth she did abyde.
      O happy herse,
Ceasse now my song, my woe now wasted is.
      O ioyfull verse.

NOVEMBER ECLOGUE 192–201

In the Dance of the Graces we saw that virtuous action itself consists in change, or rather, interchange. The two great images for world order in the Renaissance are first, a chain, or ladder of being, reaching down from God through the Angels to Man, and from him to all other created beings in their degrees, to the lowest grain of sand. This is a static view; it might be called the view of the Creator. But for the Creation the order of being is a cosmic dance. Birth, growth, death, the movement of the heavenly bodies, the interchange of the Virtues and the chorus of the Angelic Host all take part in it according to their nature. This concept is magnificently elaborated in a poem by John Davies (1569–1626) called *Orchestra*. In it Antinous woos Penelope, the wife of Ulysses, to dance. He argues that all things dance:

Dancing, bright lady, then began to be
When the first seeds whereof the world did spring,
The fire, air, earth and water, did agree
By love's persuasion, nature's mighty king,
To leave their first disordered combating
And in a dance such measure to observe
As all the world their motion should preserve.

What has thrown the earthly part of this perfect harmony of action out of time, is, of course, sin, which, as Milton says:

Jarr'd against nature's chime, and with harsh din
Broke the fair music that all creatures made
To their great Lord, whose love their motions swayed
In perfect diapason, whilst they stood
In first obedience and their state of good.

AT A SOLEMN MUSICK

In this world at its creation, the dance was complete. But Man's

Fall brought about the fall of all things beneath him on the scale of being; all the world, in fact. So, Shakespeare's Timon can see the flux of the world in terms of active corruption:

> The sun's a thief, and with his great attraction
> Robs the vast sea; the moon's an arrant thief,
> And her pale fire she snatches from the sun;
> The sea's a thief, whose liquid surge resolves
> The moon into salt tears; the earth's a thief,
> That feeds and breeds by a composture stolen
> From general excrement, each thing's a thief:
>
> TIMON OF ATHENS IV, 3, 441–7

This vision of the world, conditioned as it is by sin itself, is false and terrible. The Giant who boasts to Artegall that he can weigh the world 'equally' in his balance—that is, remould its social structure and its very elements nearer to the desire of the sinful human heart—uses this same imagery:

> He sayd that he would all the earth vptake,
> And all the sea, deuided each from either:
> So would he of the fire one ballaunce make,
> And one of th'ayre, without or wind, or wether:
> Then would he ballaunce heauen and hell together,
> And all that did within them all containe;
> Of all whose weight, he would not misse a fether.
> And looke what surplus did of each remaine,
> He would to his owne part restore the same againe....
>
> Therefore the vulgar did about him flocke, ...
> In hope by him great benefite to gaine,
> And vncontrolled freedome to obtaine.
>
> FAERIE QUEENE V, 2, 31, 33

Artegall's answer to this is uncompromising; it is a statement of the Rules of the Dance:

> All in the powre of their great Maker lie:
> All creatures must obey the voice of the most hie....
>
> He maketh Kings to sit in souerainty;
> He maketh subiects to their powre obay;
> He pulleth downe, he setteth vp on hy;

He giues to this, from that he takes away.
For all we haue is his: what he list doe, he may.

FAERIE QUEENE V, 2, 40–1

This is a magnificent statement. It is unanswerable in its own terms. But even in those terms it is not a solution. The solution can only be to see change, in time, in relation to the eternal stability of Heaven, not by way of contrast, not even as something to be transcended (as in the verse quoted above from the *November Eclogue*) in particular instances, but as part of the very process of that stability itself. This is the judgement of Nature against Mutabilitie, at the very end of the *Mutabilitie Cantos*:

I well consider all that ye haue sayd,
And find that all things stedfastnes doe hate
And changed be: yet being rightly wayd
They are not changed from their first estate;
But by their change their being doe dilate:
And turning to themselues at length againe,
Doe worke their owne perfection so by fate:
Then ouer them Change doth not rule and raigne;
But they raigne ouer change, and doe their states maintaine.

MUTABILITIE 7, 58

Virtue and beauty, all living things, grow and fulfil themselves in time, in action. Their origin, the Creator, is divine; but this creation, the process of becoming, must be completed in time, before it can have the eternal existence of Heaven to which, as its origin, it returns. Sin and corruption spoil the perfection of the 'Image of God', of the earthly manifestation of this Ideal: they make it less real, less itself. It is this imperfection which must be transcended in time; transcended and conquered.

So it is that the Dance of the Graces is only glimpsed as a vision in the Valley of the Shepherds, blessedly secluded from the struggles of the active life, where Spenser's Virtues go armed, properly to express themselves in knightly action.

4

The Faerie Queene

A detailed commentary on *The Faerie Queene* lies outside the scope of this book; my 'interpretation' of Spenser—or anybody else's—is not the purpose here. Such interpretations exist, and some of the best of them are listed in the Bibliography. This book attempts to put the reader in a position where he can form his own opinion of such interpretations. That is why, in the foregoing chapters, I have concentrated on Spenser's background, particularly his intellectual background, trying to clear away a whole area of difficulty that is basically practical in kind, relating as it does to ways of thought and kinds of learning which are generally unfamiliar today.

I have so far said very little about Spenser's poetic mastery of word and sound and image, not because these are lacking in his work—far from it—but because these qualities are easily recognisable.

It is perfectly possible to enjoy *The Faerie Queene* very much at the 'literal' level of marvellous narrative, and beautiful or terrifying description alone. I first read it like that. I was about eleven, recovering from some illness and very bored. I found a copy of Spenser—I had run out of books—and the length, far from being off-putting, was very cheering: it would last a long time—and I loved it. I got lost, and forgot who was who, but I could always be sure that something exciting would happen, or something beautiful. Odd passages stuck with me for years: the description of the two girls in the pool in Acrasia's garden particularly:

> And all the margent round about was set,
> With shady Laurell trees, thence to defend
> The sunny beames, which on the billowes bet,

And those which therein bathed, mote offend.
As *Guyon* hapned by the same to wend,
Two naked Damzelles he therein espyde,
Which therein bathing, seemed to contend,
And wrestle wantonly, ne car'd to hyde,
Their dainty parts from vew of any, which them eyde.

FAERIE QUEENE II, 12, 63

It was simply the beauty of this description which caught my
imagination: a natural response, and right, but not right enough.
For Spenser's marvellous verbal skill and music should catch the
imagination up into the delighted recognition and enjoyment of
his moral and spiritual purpose.

In this chapter I shall go through *The Faerie Queene* Book by
Book, clearing, I hope, the principal obstacles in the way of such
enjoyment as I go: no more than that. But first we will look at
the poetic form Spenser has chosen: the nine-line stanza that
bears his name.

Spenser follows Ariosto and Tasso in using a stanzaic form;
that is, he neither attempts hexameters (for which, in view of the
experiments discussed in Chapter 2, we must be very grateful)
nor takes up Surrey's 'strange metre' of blank verse, used by
him to translate Virgil. The Italian writers may have suggested
the use of stanzas rather than a more continuous form of verse,
but he does not adopt their chosen form, the *ottava rima*, (ab, ab,
ab, cc). His stanza appears to derive from an eight-line stanza,
originally developed by medieval French writers (ab, abb, cbc):
it was also used by Chaucer in *The Monk's Tale*. The debt to his
great English predecessor was probably deliberate. His elaboration of it by the addition of a ninth longer line (an Alexandrine,
with a c-rhyme in the whole verse scheme) may have been
suggested by other earlier writers: Surrey, for example, combines the Alexandrine with lines of different length, and the
effect of this may have caught Spenser's ear.

Many critics—including Dr. Johnson—have complained that
the Spenserian stanza is unsuitable for a long narrative poem:
that it is too slow-moving, and that the Alexandrine emphasises
the verse division, breaking the flow of the narrative, and that it

becomes monotonous with long reading. I disagree: to start with, Spenser's ear is very fine and there is great variety in the pace and effect of his writing. Two contrasting examples, each descriptive in kind, will serve to illustrate this without detailed analysis. The first describes a fight:

As when *Dan Æolus* in great displeasure,	1
For losse of his deare loue by *Neptune* hent,	2
Sends forth the winds out of his hidden threasure,	3
Vpon the sea to wreake his fell intent;	4
They breaking forth with rude vnruliment,	5
From all foure parts of heauen doe rage full sore,	6
And tosse the deepes, and teare the firmament,	7
And all the world confound with wide vprore,	8
As if in stead thereof they *Chaos* would restore.	9

FAERIE QUEENE IV, *9*, 23

Here the discordant, violent effect is achieved by a variety of means: particularly by the use of double consonants (especially in 1, 3, 4, 8), by combinations of words that are deliberately harsh and difficult to enunciate in sequence, ('great displeasure', 1, 'forth the', 3), and long vowels (1, 5, 6, 8), and deliberate assonance (more noticeable than alliteration which augments the effect), recalling the repeated crashing of waves, or blows (1, 4, 5, 8).

Compare this delicate verse, part of the description of the island to which Phaedria takes Guyon, tempting him into dalliance which is wrong chiefly because it distracts him from the stern activity of his quest:

It was a chosen plot of fertile land,	1
Emongst wide waues set, like a litle nest,	2
As if it had by Natures cunning hand	3
Bene choisely picked out from all the rest,	4
And laid forth for ensample of the best:	5
No daintie flowre or herbe, that growes on ground,	6
No arboret with painted blossomes drest,	7
And smelling sweet, but there it might be found	8
To bud out faire, and her sweet smels throw all around.	9

FAERIE QUEENE II, *6*, 12

Charity by Isaac Oliver, who may well have had in mind
Spenser's description of Charissa (F.Q. I, *10*, 30–31)

NICHOLAS HILLIARD

E. C. M. 1

Design for the obverse of Queen Elizabeth's Great Seal of Ireland by Nicholas Hilliard. The hands, reaching out from the clouds to support the Queen's mantle, show that divine power assists her in her exercise of royal authority. Compare the description of Mercilla (F.Q. V, 9, 27–30)

An angel displays to Henry Tudor and his family the victory of England's patron saint. Like Una (F.Q. I, *1*, 4), the princess leads her lamb, as was common in the pageants of St. George. The tower in the centre background can be compared with the description of Alma's House (F.Q. II, *9*, 22) and may be intended to have a similar symbolic significance

These trunckles heddes do playnly thowe, eache rebels farall end,
And what a haynous crime it is, the Quene for to offend.

John Derricke, in *The Image of Irelande* (1581), shows Sir Henry Sidney, father of Sir Philip, setting out from Dublin Castle on his State Progress of 1575. Note the heads of executed rebels above the gate

Here the lines flow lightly and smoothly. There is no heavy clotting of consonants; there is a clear pattern of open vowel sounds, particularly long a's (2, 3, 6, 7). There is only one word of more than two syllables ('ensample', 5), though 'choisely' might be added, and a great preponderance of monosyllabic words, especially noticeable in the Alexandrine. The whole effect is delicate and charming.

Certainly the Spenserian stanza is slow-moving as a vehicle for narrative. But for the full expression of the complex texture of allegory for which Spenser is using it, it is ideal. The possibilities it offers for climax, for pressing an argument or a description with the concluding or illuminating weight of the Alexandrine, are endless. Of these Spenser takes full advantage. It is a poetic form that greatly aids clarity of exposition, at once guiding and exciting the reader's attention at every point.

BOOK I

In the *Letter to Raleigh*, Spenser outlines the plan of the narrative framework of *The Faerie Queene*, which he never completed. Each Book is to deal with the adventures of a knight patronising a particular Virtue, and Spenser follows his models, both ancient and modern, by beginning his poem in the middle of the action. As he says:

> But because the beginning of the whole worke seemeth abrupte and as depending upon other antecedents, it needs that ye know the occasion of these . . . knights . . . aduentures. For the Methode of a Poet historical [a narrative poet], is not such, as of an Historiographer [historian]. For an Historiographer discourseth of affayres orderly as they were donne, accounting as well the times as the actions, but a Poet thrusteth into the middest, euen where it most concerneth him, and there recoursing to the thinges forepaste, and diuining of thinges to come, maketh a pleasing Analysis of all. The beginning therefore of my history, if it were told by an Historiographer, should be the twelfth booke, which is the last, where I deuise that the Faery Queene kept her Annuall feaste xii dayes, uppon which xii seuerall dayes the occasions of the xii seuerall aduentures hapned, which being vndertaken by xii seuerall knights, are in these xii books seuerally handled and discoursed.

Spenser owes this plan to the Arthurian Romances. Most of the great adventures of Arthur's knights in Malory and elsewhere begin at one of the great feasts held at his court, at Christmas or Pentecost. In the romance of *Gawain and the Greene Knight*, for example (which exists in various modernised versions), we are told that King Arthur would never sit down to the Christmas banquet before some adventure had befallen. The knights of the Court of Spenser's *Faerie Queene* take up their adventures in the same way. Spenser goes on:

> The first was this. In the beginning of the feast, there presented himselfe a tall, clownishe younge man, who falling before the Queene of Faries desired a boone (as the manner then was) which during that feast she might not refuse: which was that hee might have the atchieuement of any aduenture, which during that feaste should happen, that being graunted, he rested him on the floore, unfitte through his rusticity for a better place. Soone after entred a faire Ladye in mourning weedes, riding on a white Asse, with a dwarfe behind her leading a warlike steed, that bore the Armes of a knight, and his speare in the dwarfes hand. Shee falling before the Queene of Faeries, complayned that her father and mother an ancient King and Queene, had bene by an huge dragon many years shut up in a brasen Castle, who thence suffred them not to yssew: and therefore besought the Faery Queene to assygne her some one of her knights to take on him that exployt. Presently that clownish person vpstarting, desired that aduenture: whereat the Queene much wondering, and the Lady much gainesaying, yet he earnestly importuned his desire.

This episode is very reminiscent of the tale of Gareth and Lynet, as told by Malory, where Gareth has concealed his noble birth and, being knighted, asks to accompany Lynet to the rescue of her sister Lyonors: Lynet is much offended by his uncouth appearance and apparent meanness of station. Spenser's use of the motif is quite deliberate; it has to do with the nature of the subject of Book I—Holiness. Holiness is not a virtue, as such; it is rather a state that cannot be attained only by moral excellence, though moral and other faults impede it. The *Legend of Holiness*, while it examines and reveals what Holiness is and how it acts, is concerned on one level, that followed by the actual course of the

narrative from point to point, with the spiritual process of sanctification. Here, at the Faerie Queene's court, this process is only
beginning. The will is there, the desire for grace, but the future
champion of Holiness is untutored and uncouth.

> In the end the Lady told him that vnlesse that armour which she
> brought, would serue him (that is, the armour of a Christian man
> specified by St. Paul v. Ephesians) that he could not succeed in that
> enterprise.

St. Paul says:

> Put on the whole armour of God, that ye may be able to stand
> against the wiles of the devil. For we wrestle not against flesh and
> blood, but against principalities, against powers, against the rulers of
> the darkness of this world, against spiritual wickedness in high
> places.
>
> EPHESIANS 6, 11–12

Spenser's reference to this passage, while obvious enough, is a
clear indication that the *action* of Book I operates on the spiritual
level of allegory, though individual incidents may concentrate
their meaning on other levels, moral or political.

The 'clownishe younge man' dons the armour, 'which
being forthwith put upon him with dewe furnitures thereunto,
he seemed the goodliest man in al that company, and was well
liked of the Lady'. He is now an avowed Christian, and his virtues
and true potential become apparent. 'And eftesoones taking on
him knighthood, and mounting on that straunge Courser, he
went forth with her on that aduenture where begynneth the first
booke.'

After the prologue, in which Spenser follows Virgil at the
opening of the *Aeneid* in explaining that he has abandoned the
pastoral for the epic vein, and renews his dedication to the
Queen, the first canto opens:

> A Gentle Knight was pricking on the plaine,
> Y cladd in mightie armes and siluer shielde,
> Wherein old dints of deepe wounds did remaine,
> The cruell markes of many' a bloudy fielde;

Yet armes till that time did he neuer wield:
His angry steede did chide his foming bitt,
As much disdayning to the curbe to yield:
Full iolly knight he seemd, and faire did sitt,
As one for knightly giusts and fierce encounters fitt.

FAERIE QUEENE I, *1*, I

The proper meaning of this description of the Knight's accoutrements might be missed without reference to the *Letter to Raleigh*. The mention of the horse is important in a similar way. To a 16th-century mind the relationship between horse and rider was a natural image for the passions controlled by the will. So Antony says of his horse:

It is a creature that I teach to fight,
To wind, to stop, to run directly on,
His corporal motion governed by my spirit.

JULIUS CAESAR IV, *1*, 31

The anger of the Redcrosse Knight's horse at being curbed indicates the state of his rider: he is as yet inexperienced. His passions are not fully, willingly, under control. He will be vulnerable to certain spiritual dangers, as pride and anger and despair, and this proves true. Again, the description of Una, his companion, needs comment here:

A louely Ladie rode him faire beside,
Vpon a lowly Asse more white than snow,
Yet she much whiter, but the same did hide
Vnder a vele, that wimpled was full low,
And ouer all a blacke stole she did throw,
As one that inly mournd: so was she sad,
And heauie sat vpon her palfrey slow:
Seemed in heart some hidden care she had,
And by her in a line a milke white lambe she lad.

FAERIE QUEENE I, *1*, 4

Una is Truth, one and indivisible. She goes veiled in the world, for whose state she weeps. She needs a champion to defend her, to implement her nature by his actions. She rides on **an** ass as did Christ, and to her humility her Knight must adapt his pace and his ambition. She is innocent, but not ignorant: the partnership between her and the Knight is mutually necessary, for without her wisdom he is the victim of attack he cannot recognise. He is the Christian man, also the Church Militant, which is the guardian of Truth, and yet dependent on her.

Their first adventure is at the den of the monster Errour. The danger is at once recognised and, though the struggle is agonising and the Knight needs the constant encouragement of Una, the outcome is certain.

Almost immediately, Una and the Redcrosse Knight are separated, through the wiles of Archimago (Hypocrisy, and on the political level, the Pope), who gives them lodging and by his magic arts deceives the Knight as to Una's virtue (the nature of Truth), so that he deserts her in a passion of righteous rage.

From this point, it may be best to trace the course of the book by Spenser's treatment of its main themes. The disastrous encounter with Archimago causes the initial separation of Una and her Knight; in their subsequent adventures their natures are revealed in action, by deliberate contrast. From this moment the dangers threatening each become immediate; their limitations are shown by the very diverse ways in which they are vulnerable. Una, without the protection of her Knight (the Church and the State as institutions with doctrinal and legal power and jurisdiction), is in danger of vicious oppression. The Knight, without the companionship of Truth, whose presence is his inspiration, as her protection is his *raison d'être*, is in more subtle peril of spiritual corruption. By showing their strengths and limitations in isolation from each other, Spenser illustrates their united potential as this is finally realised in the fulfilment of the quest and the slaying of the Dragon.

Archimago's treachery brings about the separation of Una and her Knight after their first victorious encounter with Errour. The idea is that danger waits on over-confidence following first success, but, more important, it is with Archimago's appearance that the forces of evil fully engage with those of good, on every level, spiritual, intellectual and physical. The patterns initiated here apply not only to this Book; they extend throughout the poem. Certain key images and associations are introduced here, to be picked up in an infinite variety of contexts elsewhere, so providing a continuity of response in the reader. So Archimago meets his prey as night is falling, and does his deceptive work under cover of darkness. Night, for Spenser, is always associated with spiritual darkness, blindness, gloom and danger:

> The drouping Night thus creepeth on them fast,
> And the sad humour loading their eye liddes,
> As messenger of *Morpheus.* . . .

FAERIE QUEENE I, 1, 36

who, as God of Sleep, is the 'shaper', as his name means, of illusions and dreams. This theme of night as the harbinger of evil and woe is picked up constantly throughout the poem, most particularly in the description of Night herself, seen as the patroness of all evil and negation. So the witch Duessa addresses her:

> . . . let be seene,
> That dreaded *Night* in brightest day hath place,
> And can the children of faire light deface.

FAERIE QUEENE I, 5, 24

—and, when she appears:

> The messenger of death, the ghastly Owle
> With drearie shriekes did also her bewray;
> And hungry Wolues continually did howle,
> At her abhorred face, so filthy and so fowle.

FAERIE QUEENE I, 5, 30

The whole of the description is very deliberately reminiscent of the Hecate of Virgil and other classical writers; the witch-goddess and Queen of Hell.

Archimago gets Una and the Knight into his power by offering them shelter in 'a little lowly Hermitage' (I, *1*, 34) and by this, as by his 'religious' speech and behaviour, the hypocritical deceptions of the Roman Church are meant particularly. Again and again Spenser's characters find the shelter offered by small

94

dwellings under the shadow of night ominous and treacherous. The witch's hut, hidden in 'a gloomy hollow glen', where Florimell seeks refuge (III, 7, 6) is one such, and the Prince Arthur, escorting Amoret and Aemylia, finds another, the abode of Sclaunder, whose 'nature is all goodnesse to abuse' (IV, 8, 23). There are many others, all mean, and horribly inhabited.

The fortunes of Una and the Redcrosse Knight move in complementary episodes. Deprived of Truth, the Knight falls in with Duessa (double-natured, fair-seeming falsehood: her name is deliberately contrasted with that of Una). Her companion is the Pagan Knight Sans Foy, whose two brothers, Sans Loy and Sans Ioy appear elsewhere. The Knight kills him—a natural conquest—and then accepts Duessa's account of herself as Fidessa, Faith, ill-used and in need of protection (Canto 2). Her rich but tinsel trappings, and her deceptive beauty, show her to be not only Falsity but also the Church of Rome, and, on the political level, Mary Queen of Scots. Blind to all warnings, the Knight accepts her at her face value:

> And oft her kist. At length all passed feare,
> He set her on her steede, and forward forth did beare.

FAERIE QUEENE I, 2, 45

Una, seeking him alone, is recognised for what she is by the natural world; that part of it that is free from conscious wilful corruption. The lion, in accordance with the tradition that this beast respects true loyalty, follows and protects her. This is natural in her case, as the defeat of Sans Foy was natural to her Knight. As her servant he destroys Kirkrapine, the spoiler of holy things, but ignores Abessa and Corceca, who stand for religious blindness and superstition, but he dies defending her from Sans Loy, who is lawless lust and violence, the deliberate and selfish refusal of human responsibility, and she is left helpless:

> Who now is left to keepe the forlorne maid
> From raging spoile of lawlesse victors will?

FAERIE QUEENE I, 3, 43

So both find themselves in peril from which together they should have been secure.

These situations are now brought to their climax. Duessa takes the Knight to the House of Lucifera, worldly Pride. Just as small, mean dwellings may prove dangerous, so great palaces are always places of power, and glory either heavenly or false. Richness of description is common in both cases; the details are important. Here

> Such endlesse richesse, and so sumptuous shew
> Ne *Persia* selfe, the nourse of pompous pride
> Like euer saw.
>
> FAERIE QUEENE I, 4, 7

With this may be compared the terrible House of Busyrane, the sadistic and self-gratifying aspect of erotic passion, where the tapestries, for example, are

> Wouen with gold and silke so close and nere,
> That the rich metall lurked priuily
> As faining to be hid from enuious eye . . .
> Like a discoloured Snake, whose hidden snares
> Through the greene gras his long bright burnisht backe declares.
>
> FAERIE QUEENE III, 11, 28

By contrast we may take the description of the Heavenly City seen by the Redcrosse Knight from the mountain:

> Which to a goodly Citie led his vew;
> Whose wals and towres were builded high and strong
> Of perle and precious stone, that earthly tong
> Cannot describe.
>
> FAERIE QUEENE I, 10, 55

Glitter that emulates true light and splendour is one of Spenser's chief images for showing at once the falsity and the attraction of evil. Hence Lucifera's 'brightnesse'. Here the theme is developed. The Knight now beholds the procession of the Seven Deadly Sins. They pass before him, led by Lucifera who

> . . . stroue to match, in royall rich array
> Great *Iunoes* golden chaire,
>
> FAERIE QUEENE I, 4, 17

that is, she blasphemously imitates and aspires to heavenly glory in her own person. Each Sin appears diseased and hideous, according to his nature, and each rides upon an appropriate beast. Spenser is using traditional imagery here, though he elaborates upon it. The 'Processional' method of presentation is one he uses elsewhere, particularly in the descriptions of the Months, Seasons and Times that are the witnesses summoned by Mutabilitie in the *Mutabilitie Cantos*. The presentation may have been suggested by planned series of pictures, or tapestries, but Spenser uses the method to display what essentially belongs to this temporal world.

From the spell of Lucifera's glory the Knight is partly immune. It seems '. . . far vnfit for warlike swaine' (I, 4, 37). But this is no true security of spirit: it is an indication of his susceptibility to a greater peril: the danger in which he stands, which in the absence of Truth, is more than worldly corruption. The appearance of Sans Ioy, seeking vengeance for the death of Sans Foy recalls him to himself. But Duessa is there to bid him spare his foe. While she descends to Hell to find a cure for Sans Ioy's wound, he is free of her immediate influence: he can see the dungeons upon which Pride's house is founded and

> Forth ryding vnderneath the castell wall
> A donghill of dead carkases. . . .

FAERIE QUEENE I, 5, 53

he escapes—or seems to.

Una is released from Sans Loy by 'Eternall prouidence' (I, 6, 7), as her nature deserves. A troop of Fauns and Satyrs, who represent that part of mankind which being untutored is yet uncorrupt, can recognise Una for what she is as did the lion. Their faculties are greater than his, and their respect is fuller, yet erroneous: 'And made her th' Image of Idolatryes;' (I, 6, 19). Her sojourn here is a parallel to the Knight's time in the House of Pride. They are both impeded from their proper duties, but in opposite ways. He finds no spiritual scope for his passion in the House of Pride. She can work but limited good among the Satyrs. He escapes; she departs, in company with Satyrane, who though he has been brought up 'Emongst wild beasts and woods, from lawes of men exilde' (I, 6, 23) is yet of knightly lineage and nature, and so becomes her protector. Like Shakespeare, in *Cymbeline*, for example, Spenser believes strongly in the power of noble blood to assert itself under any environment, and makes varied use of this theme. But Satyrane is not proof against sophisticated cunning. Archimago distracts him into battle with Sans Loy, leaving Una to fly alone, while Satyrane can only prevent pursuit.

The last movement of their separate adventures begins. The Redcrosse Knight unarms himself; he leaves off Christian virtue and vigilance. He is no longer safe even from natural peril; drinking of an enchanted spring he loses strength and courage. This episode should be compared with that of the Well of Life and Baptism in Canto 11, 34 (see p. 60). Duessa finds him again, and he is content to dally with her, no longer needing even the pretence of knightly action. And so in this state of deadly boredom of body and spirit he falls prey to Orgoglio, spiritual pride, who imprisons him. Here to the spiritual allegory is added the political implication of the suppression of religious freedom by the Inquisition. Orgoglio then takes Duessa for his love, sitting her in the state in which the Whore of Babylon appears in the Apocalypse:

> I saw a woman sit upon a scarlet coloured beast, full of names of blasphemy, having seven heads and ten horns. And the woman was arrayed in purple and scarlet colour, and decked with gold and precious stones and pearls, having a golden cup in her hand full of abominations and filthiness of her fornication. . . . And I saw the woman drunken with the blood of the saints and with the blood of the martyrs of Jesus.
>
> REVELATION *17*, 3–6

This is in accordance with the Protestant commentaries of the time, which take the Beast with seven heads to be the city of Rome itself, and the Harlot the Papacy.

Archimago has given a false report of the death of the Redcrosse Knight, but the dwarf, escaping, tells Una the truth. She is therefore left quite helpless; she has no right hope, however faint. In this extremity she meets with Prince Arthur, who here makes his first appearance. His accoutrements are rich and war-like, and his shield of diamond invincible against all force and enchantment. He vows instantly to help her:

> But be of cheare, and comfort to you take:
> For till I haue acquit your captiue knight,
> Assure your selfe, I will you not forsake.

FAERIE QUEENE I, 7, 52

Arthur, as Magnanimity, partakes in the quest of each several Virtue. As each Virtue alone is in some way fatally vulnerable, he, as representing all, comes to the help of each in extremity. By his aid Orgoglio and Duessa are overcome; their false glamour is stripped away to reveal naked horror; the innocent blood that stains the rich halls of Orgoglio, and the age and filth of Duessa are undisguised:

> A loathly, wrinckled hag, ill fauoured, old,
> Whose secret filth good manners biddeth not be told.

FAERIE QUEENE I, 8, 46

The Redcrosse Knight is rescued, but so sick in body and spirit as to be near death:

> His pined corse, him scarse to light could beare,
> A ruefull spectacle of death and ghastly drere.

FAERIE QUEENE I, 8, 40

Their meeting, the rejoining of the two themes, is in a minor key. This is to be transposed in the House of Holiness: but first, as a refreshing contrast, and also to broaden the visionary scope of the poem as a whole, Arthur tells his story to Una, and in particular that his quest did not begin at the court of the Faerie Queene, like all the others, but must end there. For he has fallen in love with a vision of her:

> From that day forth I cast in carefull mind,
> To seeke her out with labour, and long tyne,

FAERIE QUEENE I, 9, 15

The direction of Arthur's quest moves, as it were, across that of all the others, encountering each in turn. For Beauty is Virtue's inspiration: the attainment of Beauty is its reward, seen here as operating in the sacrament of eventual marriage: an earthly and a heavenly actuality.

The quest of Arthur, and that of Una and her Knight, carry them apart as soon as Arthur's part is done:

> Thus beene they parted, *Arthur* on his way
> To seeke his loue, and th'other for to fight
> With *Vnaes* foe, that all her realme did pray.

FAERIE QUEENE I, *9*, 20

Despair is the next enemy encountered by the Knight: the spiritual reaction to his rescue from Orgoglio; and only Una's presence saves him. Till he is fully restored to himself *she* is *his* protector. The process of restoration takes place in the House of Holiness to which she brings him. Here he encounters Faith and Hope and, after the painful remedial discipline of Repentance, Charity. The whole allegory is to be contrasted with that of the House of Pride. Here there is no procession but, as we enter with Una and her Knight, there is a progressive revelation, an education in sanctity, of which the end is the vision of the Heavenly City, at once the goal of the Christian soul and the touchstone of all earthly glory. Here the Knight for the first time fully knows himself, and appropriately it is here that his specific title is revealed on the level of patriotic implication; he is St. George of England. He is ready for the final trial against the forces of darkness and evil. Up to now all has been preparation.

In one sense this is so, and the defeat of the Dragon, the Devil, is the crown of his labours. In another, it has been implied in all that has gone before: the three days' battle, which is won by the help of the sacraments of Baptism (the Well of Life) and of the Eucharist (the Tree of Life), is a re-telling in allegorical form of the trials and perils which beset the Christian life and are triumphantly overcome. In a third sense, the mystical, the Knight's battle with the Dragon is the overcoming of Hell by Christ Himself in the three days before the Resurrection. The diversity of meaning explains certain turns of the narrative: as that the Knight, on beholding the vision of the City, vows, having completed his quest, to return as a pilgrim and devote his life to no other end, although at the end of the Book he is betrothed to Una; but Una is Truth. In one sense she *is* the City. Again, the sacramental allegory of Baptism and the Eucharist is unmistakable—but before beginning this quest the Knight put on the whole armour of God. Here the battle with the Dragon is extended in meaning to cover the whole course of his life from infancy. And at the end, when the Dragon is slain and Archimago and Duessa bound, the Knight cannot wed his Una, but must return to the court of the Faerie Queene. For in this life there is no such fulfilment as brings rest. And, mystically, not until the end of the world shall Christ be finally wedded to his Bride, the new Jerusalem. Which is not to say that the triumph and the joy of victory are not real. They operate in eternity as well as in the world where they are achieved and celebrated. This is the meaning of the mysterious music heard at the betrothal feast:

> During the which there was an heauenly noise
> Heard sound through all the Pallace pleasantly,
> Like as it had bene many an Angels voice,
> Singing before th'eternall maiesty,
> In their trinall triplicities on hye;
> Yet wist no creature, whence that heauenly sweet
> Proceeded, yet each one felt secretly
> Himselfe thereby reft of his sences meet,
> And rauished with rare impression in his sprite.

FAERIE QUEENE I, *12*, 39

BOOK II

In the *Letter to Raleigh* we are told that:

> The second day ther came in a Palmer bearing an Infant with bloody hands, whose Parents he complained to haue bene slayn by an Enchauntresse called Acrasia: and therfor craued of the Faery Queene, to appoint him some knight, to perform that aduenture which being assigned to Sir Guyon, he presently went forth with that same Palmer which is the beginning of the second booke and the whole subiect thereof.

Sir Guyon is the knight portraying Temperance, and some definition of this Virtue, as Spenser thought of it, is necessary. Of all the Books of *The Faerie Queene*, this is the most directly Aristotelean, for of all the Virtues with which Spenser deals, it is the one to which his definitions are most applicable allegorically.

Aristotle classifies the Virtues as 'intellectual' and 'moral', the former belonging to the rational and the latter to the passionate parts of the soul. Where the passions are obedient to reason, liberality and temperance result; the Virtues of wisdom and prudence however are 'intellectual'. Aristotle sees temperance as necessary to prudence, and adds that intellectual virtue is the result of teaching; moral virtue of habit.

The Palmer who leads Guyon on his quest represents the intellectual aspect of the whole composite Virtue. He teaches and instructs Guyon, advising and restraining him where necessary, as in the encounter with Furor and his mother Occasion:

> With her, who so will raging *Furor* tame,
> Must first begin, and well her amenage.

FAERIE QUEENE II, *4*, 11

This function extends to his moralising quite generally on the various episodes of the story, as in his comment on Amavia's suicide:

> But temperance (said he) with golden squire
> Betwixt them both can measure out a meane,
> Neither to melt in pleasures whot desire,
> Nor fry in hartlesse griefe and dolefull teene.
> Thrise happie man, who fares them both atweene:

FAERIE QUEENE II, *1*, 58

In the course of his quest Guyon is therefore instructed both by counsel and his own experience, so that the Virtue which he portrays is in every way manifested.

Here a contrast appears with Book I, which shows the Redcrosse Knight's progression towards sanctity. Temperance is a moral Virtue: Book II shows Guyon not so much achieving it, as exercising it, as manifesting the potential of Temperance in his own nature at every range of human experience and temptation. In one sense this can be seen as a training for the final work of the quest, the overthrow of Acrasia's Bower; in another it is a detailed examination of the nature of the Virtue concerned.

Unlike Book I, the narration of Book II is not subdivided into related and contrastingly developed themes. Guyon's training takes in the ranges of temptation that attack all levels of this Virtue; those attacking the passions (anger and lust), the ambitions (greed and pride of place), and the soul (self-righteousness, self-satisfaction and sloth). This would be a modern subdivision: Spenser would use 'passions' and 'reason' to cover all these, but the terms may be useful as they help to clarify the cumulative progress of Guyon's adventures, the allegorical application of each including a higher range until temperance is manifested throughout the whole range of human faculties.

The first canto opens with Archimago's escape with Duessa, Evil, which in this world cannot be permanently chained, though individual instances of it may be destroyed. Spenser uses Archimago's escape to indicate this, as well as to give coherence to his poem as a whole. The same motif is used at the end of Book VI, when the Blatant Beast, the capture of which has been Calidore's quest, escapes:

> . . . whether wicked fate so framed,
> Or fault of men, he broke his yron chaine,
> And got into the world at liberty againe.

FAERIE QUEENE VI, *12*, 38

Archimago's initial appearance sets the note of danger awaiting Guyon, who is Virtue active and prepared. With him goes the Palmer:

> He seemd to be a sage and sober sire,
> And euer with slow pace the knight did lead,
> Who taught his trampling steed with equall steps to tread.

FAERIE QUEENE II, *1*, 7

Just as the Redcrosse Knight had to rein in his steed (the will, the passions) to keep the slower pace of Una's ass, so Guyon must restrain himself to the foot-pace of prudence.

The first attack, Archimago's attempt to set Guyon at variance with the Redcrosse Knight by playing on his generous passions, is totally unsuccessful. There follows the incident of Amavia, and here Spenser has departed from the plan outlined in the *Letter to Raleigh*. The orphaned babe, stained with its parents' blood, is rescued by Guyon in the course of his quest, not brought to the Faerie Court at its beginning. Evidently Spenser wished to have the vivid narrative impression of Acrasia's deadly power made both on Guyon and on his readers. Amavia's suicidal despair is intemperance of the passions; she serves as an example, as well as centring the motivation of Guyon's quest in the narrative action.

The Castle of Medina, to which Guyon takes the infant, is an analytical allegory of the doctrine of the Golden Mean as this was shown in the last chapter. Medina is the perfect complement to Guyon: the feminine manifestation of temperance in quietness and courtesy, restraining all violence and discord, as between her sisters' lovers and Guyon, and again between her sisters and herself.

The next canto does not directly concern Guyon's own adventures, but two characters, whose activity is to range over the whole course of the poem, make their first appearance. Both are by their nature related to Temperance: Braggadocchio (who may politically represent Alençon, Queen Elizabeth's suitor) whose boastful cowardice outrages both prudence and self-knowledge, and Belphoebe, whose lovely and independent chastity is grounded in wise restraint:

> In her faire eyes two liuing lamps did flame,
> Kindled aboue at th'heauenly makers light,
> And darted fyrie beames out of the same,
> So passing persant, and so wondrous bright,
> That quite bereau'd the rash beholders sight:
> In them the blinded god his lustfull fire
> To kindle oft assayd, but had no might;
> For with dredd Maiestie, and awfull ire,
> She broke his wanton darts, and quenched base desire.

FAERIE QUEENE II, 3, 23

She is one of the portraits of Elizabeth, the Virgin Queen; hence her likeness to Diana. More important, as independent Chastity she is an aspect of Love, and as such is developed more fully in the next two Books.

Braggadocchio steals Guyon's horse; this has a two-fold significance. Guyon must pursue his quest on foot, and Braggadocchio is revealed as aspiring to the show of noble activity for which he is in every way unworthy.

Guyon next encounters Furor, ungoverned wrath, and Occasion, and overcomes them. Furor's nature is best explained by reference to the description of Wrath as he appears in the procession of the Seven Deadly Sins in Book I:

> His ruffin raiment all was staind with blood,
> Which he had spilt, and all to rags yrent,
> Through vnaduized rashnesse woxen wood;
> For of his hands he had no gouernement,

FAERIE QUEENE I, 4, 34

Pyrochles, who wilfully unbinds Furor and Occasion, to his own pain, represents the man who goes out of his way to look for trouble: Cymochles, his brother, is the opposite extreme of sulky malevolence. Guyon is at all levels the positive mean between two negative extremes. Cymochles is found by Atin (strife) in Acrasia's bower, sunk in slothful lust: Phaedria tries to delay Guyon on his quest. She is an 'escapist', who says: 'Refuse such fruitlesse toile, and present pleasures chuse' (II, 6, 17). In this, she represents the vice that is opposed to steadfastness, which Aristotle calls 'effeminacy'; hence her sex and that of Amavia: 'It is effeminacy to fly from troubles, nor does the suicide face death because it is noble, but because it is a refuge from evil.' Acrasia's characterisation, as an evil and seductive enchantress, owes something to this conception also, as will appear.

Phaedria will not accept the Palmer in her rudderless boat, and so Guyon is separated from his guide. But this of itself does not expose him to danger, as did the Redcrosse Knight's separation from Una; he combines the Palmer's wisdom with his own active virtue. Leaving Phaedria, his next adventure is that of the cave of Mammon. So far we have been shown the reactions of Temperance to the passions, to irrational stimuli, of anger, pain and pleasure. The next episode deals first with more calculated vices—ambition and greed. Mammon sits outside his cave amid heaps of treasure: 'Great heaps of gold, that neuer could be spent' (II, 7, 5): that is, wealth kept and hoarded for its own sake, not put to its proper use of liberality. Guyon, at Mammon's invitation, enters his cave; his reactions are those of the temperate man in this world. This is not a question of a danger to be avoided, but of an attitude to be maintained. We are told that through Mammon's realm is a road: 'That streight did lead to *Plutoes* griesly raine' (II, 7, 21), that is, to Hell, and after refusing the final temptation offered by Mammon, that he should wed his daughter Ambition, Guyon follows it. Ambition is in some ways a counterpart of Lucifera in Book I. She is the worldly conception of the great chain of Degree and Order that reaches up through this earthly creation to Heaven:

> Nath'lesse most heauenly faire in deed and vew
> She by creation was, till she did fall;

FAERIE QUEENE II, 7, 45

Entering Hell, Guyon comes to the garden of Proserpina, Queen of Hell; this description is taken largely from Claudian, *The Rape of Proserpine*. It is beautiful but deadly in its peace and poisonous fertility. From here Guyon may see the rivers of Hell, and the torments of the damned. There is a seat where Mammon tempts him to rest. This is the subtlest spiritual temptation to which Temperance can be exposed: it is self-righteousness; to relax (as Temperance never can) in contemplation of the operations of divine justice upon sinners. So Dante, in Hell, pauses to listen to the cursings of the damned, and Virgil rebukes him: 'to wish to hear such things is a base desire'. It is horribly akin to the passive lasciviousness of Cymochles in Acrasia's Bower. On coming again to the upper air, Guyon swoons: his mortal strength has been unnaturally taxed. The Palmer is recalled to him by an angel, but is powerless to protect him from the passionate and powerful violence of Cymochles and Pyrochles; it is Arthur who rescues him in his extremity, supplying the limitations of Temperance with active Justice.

Guyon, Arthur and the Palmer come now to the House of Alma, the Soul, which is a complement to the Castle of Medina.

It is an elaborate allegory of the temperate soul in a perfect body, always under attack from the forces of evil. In Medina we are shown the nature of moral temperance; in Alma the soul whose activity is based upon it. Spenser is here deliberately medieval, and at his most intellectually arid: the elaborate description is only exciting as an intellectual scheme.

The description of Alma's house from outside, when Arthur, after Guyon's departure, defends it from attack, is reminiscent of the staging of the Morality Plays (which continued to be performed in England for some time after the Reformation, in some places as late as 1580). Each of the Five Senses is a bulwark attacked by horribly appropriate monsters, all under the command of Maleger:

> As pale and wan as ashes was his looke,
> His bodie leane and meagre as a rake,
> And skin all withered like a dryed rooke,
> Thereto as cold and drery as a Snake,
> That seem'd to tremble euermore, and quake:

FAERIE QUEENE II, *11*, 22

The name of this nightmare horror means 'evil sickness'; he can perhaps best be understood as Original Sin, immortal corruption. Impotence and Impatience attend him, and Arthur is at one point saved only by his squire: even Magnificence can be in debt to a meaner or slighter Virtue, or it would have no opportunity for gratitude, and so be incomplete.

The last canto falls into two parts: the approach to the Bower of Bliss, and its description and overthrow. Just as the Dragon-fight in Book I is, at one level, a recapitulation of the whole progress of the Christian Life, so this description of the voyage to the Bower is in one sense a retelling of all that has gone before in Book II. The temptations that wait upon Temperance are put into objective, 'emblematic' form (see pp. 66–7): the Gulf of Greediness, the Rock of Reproach which waits for luxurious livers, the Wandering Islands, the Quicksand of Unthriftihead. Then hideous sea-monsters attack the traveller. (Spenser has gone for their names and descriptions to the foremost writers on natural history of his day.) They are foreign and alien to the light of day, and exemplify the spiritual monstrosity to which Acrasia reduces her victims. These, and the savage flock of ill-omened birds, are calmed by the Palmer's staff which, being made of the same wood as Mercury's wand, has the power of concord that, as we saw in Medina, belongs to true Temperance. The whole voyage owes much of its descriptive detail to Homer's *Odyssey*.

The Bower itself, like its mistress, is very lovely. Otherwise it would hardly be a temptation. But its spiritual corruption appears also in its physical nature. It is artificial, in the bad sense that art has brought nature down to its own level of perverse imagination, as in the grapes of gold:

> So made by art, to beautifie the rest,
> Which did themselues emongst the leaues enfold,

FAERIE QUEENE II, *12*, 55

The counterpart to the Bower is the Garden of Adonis in the following Book: another example of the way in which Spenser extends the intellectual continuity throughout his poem. Nature has here realised her potential perfection.

> There was a pleasant arbour, not by art,
> But of the trees owne inclination made

FAERIE QUEENE III, 6, 44

Acrasia lies 'arrayd, or rather disarrayd', while a song, lifted from Tasso, bids: 'Gather the rose of love, while yet is time'; but none of Acrasia's victims do. She is no mere siren; sexual delight is too gross, too human a temptation. She is spiritual incontinence of mind and imagination; the sweet lingering melancholy of her singers is her perfect background. The effect appears in her latest victim, Verdant. His armour is put by; he has shed knightly honour and rejected its responsibilities; he is 'defaced', transformed, made less and other than himself. This voluptuous inactivity is a more profound sin than any fleshly orgy. Leisure is necessary for refreshment in this world, but no man has a *right* to it, least of all as a way of life. It is a grace only, God-given. To choose idleness implies the loss of all those faculties, of will and endeavour, reason and hope, that constitute humanity. And yet the choice can be made, for man has free will. Man can choose to reject the image of God in which he was made. This is the terrible meaning of the Palmer's comment on Grill, who refuses to have humanity restored to him when Acrasia and her works are overcome and destroyed:

> Said *Guyon*, See the mind of beastly man,
> That hath so soone forgot the excellence
> Of his creation, when he life began,
> That now he chooseth, with vile difference,
> To be a beast, and lacke intelligence.
> To whom the Palmer thus, The donghill kind
> Delights in filth and foule incontinence:
> Let *Grill* be *Grill*, and haue his hoggish mind.

FAERIE QUEENE II, 12, 87

BOOK III

This is entitled *The Legend of Britomartis, or, of Chastitie*, and in the *Letter to Raleigh* Spenser tells us:

> The third day there came in, a Groome, who complained to the Faery Queene, that a vile Enchaunter called Busirane had in hand a most faire Lady called Amoretta, whom he kept in most grieuous torment, because she would not yield him the pleasure of her body. Whereupon Sir Scudamour the louer of that Lady presently took on him that aduenture. But being vnable to performe it by reason of the hard Enchauntments, after long sorrow, in the end met with Britomartis, who succoured him and reskewed his loue.
>
> But by occasion hereof, many other aduentures are intermedled, as rather Accidents than intendments. As the loue of Britomart, the ouerthrow of Marinell, the misery of Florimell, the vertuousnes of Belphoebe, the lasciuiousnes of Hellenora, and many the like.

In Books III and IV, Spenser adopts a freer and more complex narrative pattern. Although the third Book is said to deal with Chastity and the fourth with Friendship, it would be truer to say that the subject of both is Love, in all its variety. So much is evident even from the outline given by Spenser in the Letter. The quest is that of Scudamour, but it is achieved by Britomart, Patroness of Chastity. The gracious interdependence of the Virtues, already exemplified by the aid afforded by Arthur to

Holiness and Temperance, is a central characteristic of love; part not of its limitations (Britomart needs no help from Arthur) but of its very nature. In the same way the perversions and abuses of love are introduced in all their diversity.

In these Books, Spenser draws exhaustively on the narrative invention of Ariosto, not only because the interweaving of many and varied strands fits the present plan, but also because Ariosto's romantic subject-matter and treatment accords with his immediate concerns.

Spenser's conception of Love is Platonic. In the *Hymne in Honovr of Love* he says of it:

> Such is the powre of that sweet passion,
> That it all sordid basenesse doth expell,
> And the refyned mynd doth newly fashion
> Vnto a fairer forme, which now doth dwell
> In his high thought, that would it selfe excell;
> Which he beholding still with constant sight,
> Admires the mirrour of so heauenly light.

190–6

Plato, in the *Symposium*, had seen human love, love of the beauty and then the virtue of an individual, as a step to be left behind in the way to love of Beauty and Goodness itself. But then romantic love was not invented in Plato's time. The true lover, as Spenser saw him (or her), saw Beauty itself revealed, first in the beauty of the beloved, and then more vividly in the glory added to that excellence by their own passionate appreciation of it. Since the beloved was mortal, this could be a dead end, a form of idolatry, and this is examined in the description of Cupid's Masque in the episode of the House of Busyrane, where love frustrated of its fulfilment—whether physical (by the bonds of marriage, or degree or by caprice) or spiritual (by the limitations of earthly desire)—is seen as every kind of misery and degradation.

Plato says that it is the nature of love to desire what is beloved. Aristotle says: 'It is inconsistent with the character of the Temperate man to have extravagant and wrong desires', and in this sense Britomart is temperate.

Chastity is not, for Spenser, a negative Virtue. It is a proper use of oneself, and a full use. That is why Britomart's quest for Artegall, her lover, will end in marriage, the sacramental attainment of the beloved in bodily and spiritual terms; and that is why she overcomes Guyon, the Knight of Temperance himself, when she first enters the poem in Part I. Love is divine, and all her energies are directed towards it; her passion is not below reason, as we see is the case with the victims of Acrasia and of Cupid alike; it transcends it.

Britomart is militant, active Chastity, brave and glorious. This is not a state easily achieved. Thus first pangs of her love for Artegall are described in terms of sickness:

> She wist not, silly Mayd, what she did aile,
> Yet wist, she was not well at ease perdy,
> Yet thought it was not loue, but some melancholy.
>
> FAERIE QUEENE III, 2, 27

Only the common sense of her nurse and her determined will saves her from being herself a victim of Cupid. But once her energy is controlled by will and reason and her quest begun, she is invincible.

It is also natural, in view of all that has been said about the social responsibilities inherent in this positive exercise of chastity, that her love should be Artegall, the knight whose Virtue is Justice. Aristotle says that 'friendship or love is the bond which holds states together', and that 'legislators set more store by it than by justice, for concord is akin to friendship'. Artegall, as retributive justice, is rightly complemented by Britomart:

> . . . clemence oft in things amis,
> Restraines those sterne behests, and cruell doomes of his.
>
> FAERIE QUEENE V, 7, 22

Justice is in fact a manifestation of love, so in the *Hymne of Heavenly Love* Spenser lays stress on God's justice towards the rebel angels:

> Th'Almighty seeing their so bold assay,
> Kindled the flame of his consuming yre,

And with his onely breath them blew away
From heauens hight, to which they did aspyre,
To deepest hell, . . .

85–9

Just as this relationship between the different Virtues is carefully built up throughout the poem, so the different aspects of love are interrelated. When once Britomartis and Guyon are at accord, Florimell enters the poem. As Britomartis is the faithful and invincible lover, so Florimell, to all who see her, is an object of love or lust according to their natures. Her first appearance gives the full impression of her startling radiance:

All suddenly out of the thickest brush,
Vpon a milk-white Palfrey all alone,
A goodly Ladie did foreby them rush,
Whose face did seeme as cleare as Christall stone,
And eke through feare as white as whales bone:
Her garments all were wrought of beaten gold,
And all her steed with tinsell trappings shone,
Which fled so fast, that nothing mote him hold,
And scarse them leasure gaue, her passing to behold.

FAERIE QUEENE III, 1, 15

This lovely radiance 'as a blazing starre' pursues her terrified flight throughout the Book. She is right to be afraid; her beauty is irresistible, and every encounter is fraught with possible danger. But this is not the only reason for her speed (not even Arthur can catch up with her). Her beauty makes her in some way a type, a representative of all beautiful and beloved women. She is to pure natures, the unattainable ideal: this is a function she fulfils for much of the Book. Arthur is the opposite of inconstant, when having fallen behind her wild flight:

Oft did he wish, that Lady faire mote bee
His Faery Queene, for whom he did complaine:
Or that his Faery Queene were such, as shee.

FAERIE QUEENE III, 4, 54

The rushing, visionary light cast by Florimell may be compared with the description of Britomart, unarmed in the House of Malecasta, when she is startled into indignant self-revelation by Malecasta who, deceived by her manly accoutrements, attempts to seduce her. Malecasta's knights:

> . . . saw the warlike Mayd
> All in her snow-white smocke, with locks vnbownd,
> Threatning the point of her auenging blade,
> That with so troublous terrour they were all dismayde.

FAERIE QUEENE III, 1, 63

This sudden flashing appearance is our first sight of Britomart as she naturally is: complete and invulnerable in herself. This technique, of the sudden glorious appearance of a Virtue, or of some aspect of divine beauty and goodness, is frequent in Spenser. Belphoebe's entrance (see p. 104) and Florimell's, just quoted, are other examples. Once Britomart has been revealed in her own shining vigilance, the responsibilities of her particular Virtue as these relate to marriage, the family and the State are elaborated in Merlin's prophecy that she shall be the ancestress of British Royalty. This needs some explanation, for if in one sense the glories of Britain and of England are in the future, and spring from the union of justice with pure love, yet Arthur's quest throughout the poem is the Faerie Queene, who is Glory, but also Queen Elizabeth. Two time schemes appear to operate here. Of course, time in Faerie Land is not the same as in the world. But it would be more accurate to think of time—history—as operating along a sliding scale of allegory, which allows that Britomart is not only the ancestress of British Royalty, but that Royalty itself; as such she represents the virgin militancy and active rule of Elizabeth, who is, as the true Governess of her realm, wedded to Justice.

Leaving Malecasta's house, Britomart rides on to the sea. Here she encounters Marinell. He is beloved of Florimell, but his mother, the nymph Cymoent, has warned him to beware of women's love, and he will have none of her. He is therefore a sinner against love in two ways. First, he is immature and selfish; secondly, he is introspective: his vision is turned inward, so that he cannot see, and so respond to, the divine beauty of Florimell. In this sense he is more blind than the churls who try to ravish her. He has cut himself off from the very nature of love, attempting to find security in himself. As Cymoent's son, he has charge of the 'Rich Strond' on which all the sea's treasure is cast. Britomart's reaction to the glorious sight is significantly reminiscent of Guyon's in the cave of Mammon:

> . . . she wondred much, but would not stay
> For gold, or perles, or pretious stones an howre,
> But them despised all; for all was in her powre.
>
> FAERIE QUEENE III, 4, 18

This treasure stands for love and beauty, all of which are laid at Marinell's feet, but which his lack of response renders useless and unenjoyed. He is overthrown by Britomart; this wound, this pain he suffers is necessary to his cure, and the incident is described in terms of a sacrifice:

> Like as the sacred Oxe, that carelesse stands,
> With gilden hornes, and flowry girlonds, crownd,
> Proud of his dying honor and deare bands,
> Whiles th'altars fume with frankincense arownd,
> All suddenly with mortall stroke astownd,
> Doth groueling fall, . . .
>
> FAERIE QUEENE III, 4, 17

—a heathen sacrifice, for Marinell's self-love is a kind of idolatry.

The entrance of Marinell introduces the development of Florimell's adventures, while Britomart passes out of the narrative for a time. Among those who follow Florimell is Timias, Arthur's squire. He is wounded by three 'fosters' and succoured by Belphoebe, who lives like Diana in the woods with her maidens.

Belphoebe is virginal Chastity, independent and self-reliant; she has no concern with the love that Timias begins to feel for her:

> But that sweet Cordiall, which can restore
> A loue-sick hart, she did to him enuy;
>
> FAERIE QUEENE III, 5, 50

The resolution of this situation is fitly left to the following Book, which deals with that kind of love which is called friendship—a much feebler word today than it was in Spenser's time.

Belphoebe is the twin sister of Amoretta. Both are born through the pure generation of the Sun, type of celestial light and beauty:

> Pure and vnspotted from all loathly crime,
> That is ingenerate in fleshly slime.

FAERIE QUEENE III, 6, 3

—of the virgin nymph Chrysogonee. They are twin aspects of Love itself, derived from its single divine original. They are brought up by Diana and Venus, whose age-old rivalry is resolved. From opposites, they become complementary aspects of the activity of love: constant virginity and faithful and fruitful marriage.

Venus takes the infant Amoretta to the Garden of Adonis, which in its fresh and living beauty is a direct contrast to Acrasia's Bower. The allegory here is very difficult; it is one of the very few places where Spenser's thought seems not to have been altogether clear. But, briefly, it is:

> . . . the first seminarie
> Of all things, that are borne to liue and die,

FAERIE QUEENE III, 6, 30

> Infinite shapes of creatures there are bred,

FAERIE QUEENE III, 6, 35

—and these shapes are drawn out of unformed chaos:

> All things from thence doe their first being fetch,
> And borrow matter.

FAERIE QUEENE III, 6, 37

Spenser seems here to have taken from Augustine the idea that all created things that ever should be were formed in the mind of God before the creation of the world, before they began to appear in the course of time. To this he allies the Platonic conception of *forms*: the various creation, derived from the eternal Ideas or 'substance' of every kind, expressed in matter:

> The substance is not chaunged, nor altered,
> But th'only forme and outward fashion; . . .
> For formes are variable and decay,
> By course of kind, and by occasion;

FAERIE QUEENE III, 6, 38

It is these forms, rather than the souls which inhabit them, which go into the world, and return, to grow afresh:

> . . . as they had neuer seene
> Fleshly corruption, nor mortall paine.

FAERIE QUEENE III, 6, 33

So that though here there is no sin, yet, as fits the presence of Venus and Adonis (who are, in Neo-Platonic allegory, Matter and Form themselves), love is fine and fruitful:

> Franckly each paramour his leman knowes,
> Each bird his mate, ne any does enuie
> Their goodly meriment, and gay felicitie.

FAERIE QUEENE III, 6, 41

—yet 'Time their troubler is', because this garden supplies the created world with forms that grow and decay.

The pure and sinless birth of Love, in its two manifestations of virginity and womanliness, is thrown into strong relief by the contrasting description of Argante and Ollyphant in the following canto: giants born incestuously from the earth, and living in monstrous and malignant sin 'gainst natures law' (III, 7, 49).

Lust is every way unnatural, uncreative and destructive; it lies in wait for all who are weak or unwary in love. These monsters are a horrible parody of Belphoebe and Amoret. In the next canto another kind of false love is introduced, in the false Florimell, the snowy image made by the witch to comfort her son after Florimell's escape. The making of this image may be compared to the shape in the likeness of Una made by Archimago to deceive the Redcrosse Knight (I, 1, 45). The snowy Florimell is not, however, intended to do active harm: her evil nature consists simply in her not being the real thing. When she appears, she deceives all who behold her.

The next illustration of the perversions of love is that of sexual jealousy in the episode of Malbecco and Hellenore, in whose house Britomart and Paridell (the wanton, courtly lover) seek shelter. Malbecco is the old, possessive husband of a young and wanton wife. His jealousy is justified in that she is unfaithful: Spenser wants his comment on the sin of jealousy to be uncomplicated by its being, like Othello's, causeless. Hellenore and Paridell have all the fashionable tricks, learnt from Ovid's *Art of Loving*, that Renaissance handbook to graceful seduction:

> Thenceforth to her he sought to intimate
> His inward griefe, by meanes to him well knowne,
> Now *Bacchus* fruit out of the siluer plate
> He on the table dasht, as ouerthrowne,
> Or of the fruitfull liquor ouerflowne,
> And by the dauncing bubbles did diuine,
> Or therein write to let his loue be showne;
> Which well she red out of the learned line,
> A sacrament prophane in mistery of wine.

> FAERIE QUEENE III, *9*, 30

Hellenore elopes with Paridell: he casts her off, and she finds her natural level among 'the iolly *Satyres* full of fresh delight . . .' (III, *10*, 44), that is, she rejects all human responsibilities. She is content; that she is so is all Spenser's judgement upon her. But Malbecco, failing to persuade her to return to the perversion of human society that is their marriage, flees from the satyrs, and his jealousy consumes him; like Envy, of which his sin is the sexual manifestation, he feeds on poisonous reptiles, and from being diseased, he has become the disease itself; all humanity is gone; he:

> Is woxen so deform'd, that he has quight
> Forgot he was a man, and *Gealosie* is hight.

> FAERIE QUEENE III, *10*, 60

Continuing on her way, Britomart encounters Scudamour, so picking up the main thread of the quest outlined in the *Letter to Raleigh*. The House of Busyrane, where Amoret, stolen from Scudamour on their wedding day, is imprisoned in dreadful pain, is the culminating allegory of perverted and false love. Scudamour, whose heraldic device is Cupid, loves Amoret truly but not faultlessly: his uncontrolled despair is one indication of this:

> Faire *Amoret* must dwell in wicked chaines,
> And *Scudamore* here dye with sorrowing.

FAERIE QUEENE III, 11, 24

for he cannot pass the barrier of smoke and fire—emblem of corrupted passion—that lies before Busyrane's house. These indications of possessive passion are important. Britomart enters without difficulty. She finds the first room, which is hung about with tapestries. These show episodes from the loves of the Gods: Leda and the Swan, Ganymede and the Eagle. The Gods themselves are the victims of Cupid: like Acrasia's lovers; they are transformed from their proper shapes and natures. Here there is an altar, with an idol of Cupid standing above a blinded dragon, whose significance can best be seen by reference to Milton. In *Comus*, the second brother says:

> But beauty like the fair Hisperian Tree
> Laden with blooming gold, had need the guard
> Of Dragon watch with uninchanted eye,
> To save her blossoms, and defend her fruit,
> From the rash hand of bold Incontinence.

393–7

Cupid's dragon is Morality. Its humiliation is essential to his triumph.

The second room is all of wrought gold, hung with trophies and armour. These are signs of a more profound triumph. Cupid has the power to unmake men, by distracting them from their proper sphere. So, in one of his sonnets, Sidney complains that his love for Stella has made him fail in his public duties.

All is empty, silent and oppressive. Britomart waits, armed, till nightfall. Then there is wind and storm, and from the third room, locked until now, there enters the Masque of Cupid. First come Fancy, Desire, Fear, Suspicion: all the attendant ills of unfulfilled love. The last, Cruelty, leads Amoret, bleeding, her heart in a silver basin transfixed with a dart, half dead. We remember that her marriage was unconsummated: this explains her position in the procession. Cupid follows:

> That man and beast with powre imperious
> Subdeweth to his kingdome tyrannous:

FAERIE QUEENE III, *12*, 22

He has left off his blindfold, to enjoy his '. . . spoyle of that same dolorous Faire Dame . . .' (III, *12*, 22).

After 'the expense of passion' comes 'the waste of Shame'. Cupid is followed by Reproach, Repentance, Shame and so on to Death: the ills that wait on the fulfilment of illegitimate love. Then all depart. Britomart waits again till nightfall. The door opens. She enters the third room. There is only Amoret, bleeding, bound to a pillar, with Busyrane:

> And her before the vile Enchaunter sate,
> Figuring straunge characters of his art,
> With liuing bloud he those characters wrate,
> Dreadfully dropping from her dying hart,
> Seeming transfixed with a cruell dart,
> And all perforce to make her him to loue.

FAERIE QUEENE III, *12*, 31

Britomart overcomes him, forces him to restore Amoret, and delivers her from the now ruined palace.

Busyrane, whose name appears to come from Busiris, an Egyptian king famous for cruelty, is found only in the inmost room. The outer room is where false Love is worshipped, and his triumph is there shown as delightful. The second room displays his true nature, his activity in terms of human suffering. This is his triumph still, but not tempting to his victims as it is portrayed. In the third room, Busyrane himself dwells, the 'Enchaunter', the very principle of perversion. All the rest emanates from him and depends on him. It is his house. The description of the ceremonies held there are derived not only from the conventional allegories of courtly, adulterous love, but also, as the mysterious procession, the tempest, the strange wound of Amoret, from such legends as that of the Graal. The ritual is not merely that of lust, but of the perversion of spiritual yearning. On that level Busyrane desires to possess not merely Amoret's body, but the heavenly perfection which is manifest in her beauty and virtue. Lust of the spirit drags down divine loveliness from Heaven itself. It cannot be destroyed; Amoret does not die. It can only suffer. Perhaps it cannot do that unless there is some mortal flaw—in Amoret's case it may be no more than ignorance and inexperience—on which Busyrane can seize. He is taking advantage of the frailty of the human condition to tyrannise over what is divine in it: virtue and beauty. And Spenser presents this ultimate perversity in terms of ritual sadism. At least that is my reading of the allegory. This is, one must say in fairness, one of the most disputed passages in Spenser's work.

The third Book has two endings. The first gives the reconciliation between Amoret and Scudamour. In the second, rewritten so as to lead straight into the plan of the following Book, Britomart finds that Scudamour has departed, and she is left with Amoret in her protection.

BOOK IV

The *Letter to Raleigh* deals only with the first three Books, so we now have no exterior guide. Book IV has as its subject Friendship. For this, it may be as well to take Spenser's own definition, which expresses the general opinion of his time.

> Hard is the doubt, and difficult to deeme,
> When all three kinds of loue together meet,
> And doe dispart the hart with powre extreme,
> Whether shall weigh the balance downe; to weet
> The deare affection vnto kindred sweet,
> Or raging fire of loue to woman kind,
> Or zeale of friends combyned with vertues meet.
> But of them all the band of vertuous mind
> Me seemes the gentle hart should most assured bind.
>
> For naturall affection soone doth cesse,
> And quenched is with *Cupids* greater flame:
> But faithfull friendship doth them both suppresse,
> And them with maystring discipline doth tame,

Through thoughts aspyring to eternall fame.
For as the soule doth rule the earthly masse,
And all the seruice of the bodie frame,
So loue of soule doth loue of bodie passe,
No lesse than perfect gold surmounts the meanest brasse.

FAERIE QUEENE IV, 9, 1–2

The mention of Cupid is important here. Love such as that of Britomart for Artegall of course *includes* friendship in this sense.

Friendship is the most diverse form of love, and so this Book has more characters than any other: more meetings, encounters, jousts, to give opportunity for expressing its every nuance, false and true, as well as the vicissitudes it may undergo. We may first examine some of the ideas concerning friendship which were familiar to Spenser and his contemporaries from their reading of Aristotle, Cicero and other authors, ancient and modern, but which are less clear to a modern reader, before seeing how the whole theme of the Book is expressed in universal terms.

The verses just quoted show that the idea of equality in friendship is important to Spenser: in perfect friendship men should give and take on equal terms. Where friendship is unequal (as in Britomart's protection of Amoret), the stronger partner receives honour, the weaker, help. This idea is elaborated in the episode of Cambel, and his joust with the three sons of Agape, Priamond, Diamond and Triamond.

Agape is the Greek for what the biblical translators usually render as 'Charity'; the highest because least self-seeking form of love, directed without distinction to all mankind. Her sons are all good knights, but not complete in excellence. Just as the Three Graces are derived from the single Venus, and form a triad, a threefold expression of her nature, so Agape's sons were:

As if but one soule in them all did dwell,
Which did her powre into three parts diuyde;
Like three faire branches budding farre and wide,
That from one roote deriu'd their vitall sap:
And like that roote that doth her life diuide,
Their mother was,

FAERIE QUEENE IV, 2, 43

As sons, they together express the masculine potential of Agape's nature: the qualities that together make up a worthy friend, though here they are divided between three individuals. But Agape obtains from the Fates a boon, that when the eldest dies:

> Eftsoones his life may passe into the next;
> And when the next shall likewise ended bee,
> That both their liues may likewise be annext
> Vnto the third, that his may so be trebly wext.

FAERIE QUEENE IV, 2, 52

When the three brothers challenge Cambell to joust for the love of Canacee, this gift takes effect. Priamond and Diamond are slain, and Triamond, to whose nature their qualities have been added, is left fighting with Cambell. They are every way equal: the battle is a complete deadlock; until at last:

> So both at once fell dead vpon the field,
> And each to other seemd the victorie to yield.

FAERIE QUEENE IV, 3, 34

This is the negative manifestation of their equality. Cambina (Concord), the daughter of Agape, sister of Triamond, intervenes to change it into its positive form. She enters in a chariot drawn by lions, and her power and nature is shown by the fact that they are: 'Now made forget their former cruell mood' (IV, 3, 39). She is beautiful as an angel: her power is heavenly. She carries a 'rod of peace':

> About the which two Serpents weren wound,
> Entrayled mutually in louely lore,

FAERIE QUEENE IV, 3, 42

or *caduceus*, such as that with which Mercury subdues the fiends of Hell. This recalls the powers of the Palmer's rod over Acrasia's monsters (II, 12, 41) and Mercury's own use of his authority over the Titaness, Mutabilitie herself (*Mutabilitie 6*, 18). Cambina carries a cup of Nepenthe which has the power to assuage all resentment. By the power of these divine instruments she restores peace and initiates friendship:

Instead of strokes, each other kissed glad,
And louely haulst from feare of treason free,
And plighted hands for euer friends to be.

FAERIE QUEENE IV, *3*, 49

Cambell's marriage with Canacee, the cause of the original strife,
and Priamond's to Cambina, crowns this relationship by placing
it in the wider context of family responsibility.

After this extremely compressed allegorical episode, there
succeeds a discursive treatment of the tournaments that follow.
The false, snowy Florimell, whose physical beauty is unenlivened
by the divine fire of mind and spirit, and who is a fatal allure to
all who see and admire her, is there with Braggadocchio, appropriately enough; and Satyrane, who has found the girdle
dropped by the true Florimell in her flight, which none but she
can wear, and many others, including Britomart who here at
last unknowingly encounters Artegall, and overthrows him, for
so this first, modest reaction of Chastity repels even true love.
Britomart appears as the protector of Amoret—whose nature,
of the same pure quality as Florimell's, allows her alone of all
those present, to wear the girdle.

The narrative widens to show the disharmonies that wait even
on true love and friendship. Scudamour, provoked by Ate
(Discord), is jealous of Britomart's friendship for Amoret (not
knowing her to be a woman), and that dangerously uncontrolled
element in his love for Amoret which prevented his rescuing her
in the previous Book shows itself in his vulnerability to suspicion
and enmity; the implications of this extend when he prevails
on Artegall to take his part against Britomart. He overthrows
her, as no other knight would be capable of doing. But at the
sight of her beauty the first effects of true love are felt. He:

> . . . felt some ruth, or sence his hand did lacke,
> Or both of them did thinke, obedience
> To doe to so diuine a beauties excellence. . . .
>
> And of his wonder made religion,
> Weening some heauenly goddesse he did see, . . .

FAERIE QUEENE IV, *6*, 21–2

But the recognition, and exchange of vows that follows this proves itself an opportunity for evil to work. Amoret, from whom Britomart's protective attention has been distracted, wanders away and falls into the hands of Lust, from which she is saved by Timias who is still living under Belphoebe's care.

Both Amoret and Belphoebe are shown by Spenser as very inexperienced, and Amoret's fears and the intolerance to which Belphoebe is prone, are the only faults in their immaculate natures; they have to learn by experience how to be fully themselves. Amoret's proper fulfilment lies in marriage, and Belphoebe learns, by her relationship with Timias that her virginity does not involve a rejection of love, but fits that mature form of it which consists in comradeship. (In Spenser's analysis of love and friendship quoted at the beginning of this section, friendship is the successor of sexual love.)

Prince Arthur's part in this Book, which follows on this episode, is less clear-cut, because of the nature of the Virtue concerned. In his rescue of Amoret and Aemylia, the immunity of himself and those associated with him from slander, and his destruction of Corflambo (passionate lust) as well as in the advice and help he gives to Poeana and her lover, he shows the effects of friendship, not only as a particular relationship, but as a quality of mind. It is he who reconciles Britomart and Scudamour, so exercising the power of concord exemplified earlier by Cambina. This gives Scudamour the opportunity to tell the story of his journey to Venus' Temple to find Amoret, before Busyrane first took her from him.

The Temple of Venus is a direct contrast to that of the House of Busyrane. It is set in the fourth Book, because Venus here is more than the Goddess of sexual love. She presides over all kinds of love:

> . . . she hath both kinds in one,
> Both male and female, both vnder one name:
> She syre and mother is her selfe alone,
> Begets and eke conceiues, ne needeth other none.

FAERIE QUEENE IV, *10*, 41

On the physical level, she presides over generation and fruitfulness in the earth: this is the effect in the created world of that part of her nature which is shown by the allegory of the Garden of Adonis in the third Book. The hymn which is sung to her expresses this: it is drawn almost exactly from the Invocation to Venus as the generative force in nature with which Lucretius begins his poem *De Rerum Natura*:

> So all the world by thee at first was made,
> And dayly yet thou doest the same repayre:
> Ne ought on earth that merry is and glad,
> Ne ought on earth that louely is and fayre,
> But thou the same for pleasure didst prepayre.
>
> FAERIE QUEENE IV, *10*, 47

According to the idea that the human (rational) soul includes the faculties of animal soul (will and appetite) as these in turn include those of plants (growth) and minerals (being, attraction and repulsion), so the fruitful power of Venus extends to the love of soul as well as that of body. The '. . . flocke of little loues, and sports, and ioyes' (IV, *10*, 42) that play about her like angels should be compared with Charity's many children:

> A multitude of babes about her hong,
> Playing their sports, that ioyd her to behold,
>
> FAERIE QUEENE I, *10*, 31

Spenser's image of Charity expresses spiritual fruitfulness in terms of marriage and children. His Venus manifests creative power in terms of the 'little loves', the fair effects of her power in the soul. In both cases, creative, generative power is the motive of the allegory.

Venus' power is beneficent, but its effects vary according to the individual's response. Her victims are too often like Cupid's in the House of Busyrane:

> Great sorts of louers piteously complayning,
> Some of their losse, some of their loues delay,
> Some of their pride, some paragons disdayning,
> Some fearing fraud, some fraudulently fayning
>
> FAERIE QUEENE IV, *10*, 43

Like all power, that of Venus is perilous if mishandled. So Scudamour, though he achieves free access to Amoret as her true lover, is, as we know, guilty of faults of passion. And Amoret, although 'Shyning with beauties light, and heauenly vertues grace' (IV, *10*, 52) is yet dependent and vulnerable to fear. In entering the Temple and approaching Amoret, Scudamour encounters those hazards of first love that, carried to their negative extreme, have their proper place in the first part of the Masque of Cupid: Doubt, Delay, Daunger. But Scudamour, unlike Cupid's victims, enters through the Gate of Good Desert into the precincts of Venus, where all is fresh and lovely as in the Garden of Adonis:

> It seem'd a second paradise to ghesse,
> So lauishly enricht with natures threasure,

FAERIE QUEENE IV, 10, 23

—where all lovers made famous in legend and story, and also those famous for noble friendship, properly enjoy love. On the steps of the Temple itself are Love and Hatred, whose close relationship has been shown in the episode of Triamond and Cambell: governed here, as then, by Concord:

> Mother of blessed *Peace* and *Friendship* trew; . . .
> The which right well her workes diuine did shew:
> For strength, and wealth, and happinesse she lends,
> And strife, and warre, and anger does subdew:

FAERIE QUEENE IV, 10, 34

In taking Amoret from the lap of Womanhood and wooing her to be his wife, Scudamour shows the proper direction of erotic passion: this is its way to sanctification, instead of the frustrated agony of Busyrane's house:

> . . . it fitteth best
> For *Cupids* man with *Venus* mayd to hold.

FAERIE QUEENE IV, 10, 54

The narrative then shifts, by way of recalling the fate of the true Florimell, now a prisoner of the Sea God, Proteus, to the fullest expression of the theme of the Book: the marriage between

the Rivers Thames and Medway, where the elements themselves
join to express ceremonially the theme of Concord:

> . . . the famous riuers came,
> Which doe the earth enrich and beautifie:

FAERIE QUEENE IV, 11, 20

and the bride in all her beauty:

> Her goodly lockes adowne her backe did flow
> Vnto her waste, with flowres bescattered, . . .

FAERIE QUEENE IV, 11, 46

—is attended by her tributary streams, and by the sea-nymphs,
including Cymodoce, as Cymoent, the mother of Marinell is
here called. Her presence is important. For it is after she has
partaken in this glorious solemnity that Marinell, who has heard
the complaints of the imprisoned Florimell, moved by pity, has
come at last to value her love. He pleads with his mother, and
she obtains Florimell's freedom:

> And was right ioyous, that she gotten had
> So faire a wife for her sonne *Marinell*.

FAERIE QUEEN IV, 12, 33

The first effect of his new love for Florimell has been misery and
sickness (the effect of frustrated passion; but more important, of
frustrated pity for her). But seeing her beauty he recovers:

> Who soone as he beheld that angels face,
> Adorn'd with all diuine perfection,
> His cheared heart eftsoones away gan chace
> Sad death, reuiued with her sweet inspection,
> And feeble spirit inly felt refection;
> As withered weed through cruell winters tine,
> That feeles the warmth of sunny beames reflection,
> Liftes vp his head, that did before decline
> And gins to spread his leafe before the faire sunshine.

FAERIE QUEENE IV, 12, 34

BOOK V

In the fifth Book, containing the Legend of Artegall or Justice,

Spenser returns to the plan of the first two Books: a single quest, pursuing an uncomplicated course.

To Spenser, Justice was the chief of all the Virtues: unless Justice was maintained, the others could not flourish:

> Most sacred vertue she of all the rest,
> Resembling God in his imperiall might;
> Whose soueraine powre is herein most exprest,
> That both to good and bad he dealeth right,
> And all his workes with Iustice hath bedight.
> That powre he also doth to Princes lend,
> And makes them like himselfe in glorious sight,
> To sit in his owne seate, his cause to end,
> And rule his people right, as he doth recommend.
>
> FAERIE QUEENE V, Prol. 10

The justice of God in the physical and social make-up of this created world is illustrated in the episode of the Giant (see p. 84). This is the divine manifestation of that kind of justice called distributive. Aristotle says that what is unjust in this sense may be called unfair, and that this kind of justice may be seen as 'a kind of proportion'. It applies to social structures, as well as criminal or violent behaviour arising from greed, and other passions which lead to the violation of right values and fair dealing. The first part of this Book deals with Artegall as the instrument of distributive justice. Spenser tells us that he was brought up and trained by Astraea, Goddess of Justice, and the last of the Gods to leave the world at the end of the Golden Age. She taught him the operations of justice in the natural world:

> She caused him to make experience
> Vpon wyld beasts, which she in woods did find,
> With wrongfull powre oppressing others of their kind.
>
> FAERIE QUEENE V, 1, 7

She gives to him the sword Chrysaor, with which Jove overcame the rebellious Giants. Here Spenser is again drawing directly on Ariosto. On leaving this world, she left him her 'groome':

> His name was *Talus*, made of yron mould,
> Immoueable, resistlesse,
>
> FAERIE QUEENE V, 1, 12

—who stands for the force necessary to the implementation of justice in a fallen world. We are told that Artegall's particular quest:

> . . . was to succour a distressed Dame,
> Whom a strong tyrant did vniustly thrall,
> And from the heritage, which she did clame,
> Did with strong hand withhold: *Grantorto* was his name.
>
> FAERIE QUEENE V, *1*, 3

The fulfilment of this quest is the culminating illustration of justice: it belongs in kind to Aristotle's retributive justice.

His first adventure is his meeting with Sangliere, who is guilty of murderous anger. This is not a fault that can be corrected: it can only be punished, but the terms of Artegall's sentence are such as to restore moral proportion:

> And you, Sir Knight, that loue so light esteeme,
> As that ye would for little leaue the same,
> Take here your owne, that doth you best beseeme,
> And with it beare the burden of defame;
> Your owne dead Ladies head, to tell abroad your shame.
>
> FAERIE QUEENE V, *1*, 28

His next encounter, with Munera, whose greed has made her richer than many princes, and who guards her wealth with murderous ungenerosity, is more interesting. He does not, as one would expect, enforce the just redistribution of her gains.

> But he her suppliant hands, those hands of gold,
> And eke her feete, those feete of siluer trye,
> Which sought vnrighteousnesse, and iustice sold,
> Chopt off, and nayld on high, that all might them behold.
>
> FAERIE QUEENE V, *2*, 26

He then drowns her, and destroys her castle with all the riches it contains. Both here and in the preceding adventure, *exemplary* justice seems to take precedence of the distributive element. The reasons for this will be considered presently. Next comes the encounter with the Giant, the central allegory of this aspect of justice.

There follows the account of the tournament held to celebrate the marriage of Florimell and Marinell. Here Artegall is seen as presiding over that aspect of distributive justice which consists in a right sense of values; of seeing things as they truly are. He sets the true Florimell beside her snowy image, which instantly dissolves:

> Ne of that goodly hew remayned ought,
> But th' emptie girdle, which about her wast was wrought.
>
> FAERIE QUEENE V, 3, 24

Artegall also completes Braggadocchio's disgrace (for he had been champion of the false Florimell) by restoring to Guyon the horse he had stolen from him (II, 3) and causing Talus to strip him of the knightly accoutrements he is unworthy to carry.

Continuing on his quest, Artegall resolves the dispute between Amidas and Bracidas, showing how justice is related to concord:

> So was their discord by this doome appeased,
> And each one had his right.
>
> FAERIE QUEENE V, 4, 20

Rescuing Terpin from the Amazons, he hears of Radigund: 'A Princesse of great powre, and greater pride' (V, 4, 33) who wars against men, and humiliates her captives, dressing them in women's clothing, and forcing them to do women's work. Artegall vows to punish her and the Book moves into its second phase, that dealing with retributive justice. In his duel with Radigund, Artegall commits one of the possible faults of this kind of justice: pity, or laxity. Radigund's beauty moves him to unmerited compassion, and he becomes her degraded thrall, not through her strength, but his own weakness.

> So was he ouercome, not ouercome,
> But to her yeelded of his owne accord;
> Yet was he iustly damned by the doome
> Of his owne mouth, that spake so wareless word,
> To be her thrall, and seruice her afford.
>
> FAERIE QUEENE V, 5, 17

Here two things must be clearly understood. First, Radigund's kingdom, by its reversal of the natural functions and activities of the sexes, is as offensive to created order as to civil decency and concord. (The political allegory, which is most prominent in this Book, indicates that Radigund, the false queen, is Mary Queen of Scots.) Secondly, when Britomart is told by Talus of Artegall's plight, she rescues him, killing Radigund without mercy; not out of jealousy, but to restore him to himself. So the first act of retributive justice in this Book is carried out, not by Artegall but by Britomart. On the political level, although Lord Grey sat on the tribunal that tried Mary, it was of course Elizabeth who signed the death warrant, though with a reluctance of which no illustration is here given. Spenser makes more of this when describing Mercilla's grief when she is forced to condemn Duessa, who is again Mary. More important, the incident shows the complexity of justice itself. In her vision in the Church of Isis, before she reaches the Amazon Kingdom, Britomart sees herself restraining the 'stern behests' of Artegall: she is equity, and this to Spenser means also mercy. Without equity, justice is incomplete, and we are told nothing of Artegall's adventures before his first meeting with Britomart: they do not form part of his quest. But laxity is not mercy, or any kind of equity; Britomart's dealings with Radigund make that clear.

It is significant that Artegall is nowhere shown as falling into the opposite fault to laxity: barbarous severity. Spenser chose to use as the great example of justice a contemporary situation: Lord Grey's administration in Ireland. In seeing Grey's severity as just, Spenser was not in agreement with all his contemporaries, and quite apart from the interpretation he might put upon certain kinds of repressive measure, he was concerned to show Artegall (Lord Grey) in a light that gave no scope for criticism on that score. He is in fact writing on the defensive, as a result of tying his allegory so closely to events about which he felt strongly and emotionally, and it is this which makes the allegory of the last part of this Book less satisfactory, because it is less free and consistent than anything else in his work.

The overthrow of the Souldan and of Adicia his wife by Artegall and Arthur refers to the international politics of the time, in particular to Elizabeth's attempted negotiations with Spain, and this can be worked out in some detail. But the more general application of the episode shows, in the fate of Adicia (whose name means Injustice), that retributive justice, once set in motion, takes its own course. Adicia's passionate anger is such:

> . . . that she transformed was
> Into a Tygre, and that Tygres scath
> In crueltie and outrage she did pas,
> To proue her surname true, that she imposed has.

FAERIE QUEENE V, *8*, 49

The narrative now shifts to Ireland, and after his encounter with Guyle, Artegall comes to the Palace of Mercilla, the figure of Elizabeth's Royal Justice (see the illustration between pp. 88–9). She sits in regal majesty: angels play about her garments, the emanations of the divine power of mercy which she wields. They are reminiscent again of the children of Charity, and the little Loves of Venus. She is attended by Justice, Order, Peace, the Daughters of Law (another Triad, like the Graces), by Temperance and Reverence. And yet, alone among Spenser's shining Virtues, her glory seems contrived. Her mercy seems too petty for its magnificent context: at least, through the opportunities she is given by Spenser to display it.

There follows the trial and condemnation of Duessa (Mary Queen of Scots), and the complaint of Belge (the Netherlands) against (Spanish) aggression. Arthur vows to reinstate Belge to her right, and in due course does so, slaying Gerioneo (who must represent the Prince of Parma, the Spanish Regent of the Netherlands) and overthrowing the idol to which he has made human sacrifice (the Inquisition), and the horrible monster that emerges from beneath the altar. This sickening beast is reminiscent of Errour (I, *1*) and is the misuse of the intellect to convince in a wrong cause:

> . . . many a one, which came vnto her schoole
> Whom she did put to death, deceiued like a foole.

FAERIE QUEENE V, *11*, 25

The historical allegory here refers to Leicester's campaign in the Netherlands: it expresses rather its wished-for outcome than the actual, inconclusive, event. Or it can be seen as a hopeful prophecy.

Artegall leaves Mercilla's court and completes his quest. He saves Irena from death, and kills the Tyrant Grantorto. Spenser has given artistic finality to the campaign of Lord Grey in Ireland (particularly by using as a central motive his massacre in 1580 of the foreign mercenaries whose expedition, led by Fitzmaurice and the Legate Dr. Sanders, held the Papal Commission). It is probably more correct to identify Grantorto with the Pope than, as is more common, with Philip of Spain, who had no hand in the Irish situation. Artegall restores Irena to her right, and:

> During which time, that he did there remaine,
> His studie was true Iustice how to deale,
> And day and night employ'd his busie paine
> How to reforme that ragged common-weale:
> And that same yron man which could reueale
> All hidden crimes, through all that realme he sent,
> To search out those, that vsd to rob and steale,
> Or did rebell gainst lawful gouernment;
> On whom he did inflict most grieuous punishment.

FAERIE QUEENE V, 12, 26

This is a fair description of Grey's administration. It is doubtful whether any individual, in any actual situation, could provide a satisfactory image for a Virtue if he were taken as so close a model as this. That this is so noticeable in this Book is partly due to the faults of the model.

The Book ends on a note of inconclusive disillusionment. Like Grey, Artegall is recalled to the court of the Faerie Queene, and on his way is horribly attacked by Enuie and Detraction, and:

> Thereto the Blatant beast by them set on
> At him began aloud to barke and bay,
> With bitter rage and fell contention.

FAERIE QUEENE V, 12, 41

The Sixth Book, the legend of Calidore, or Courtesy, should be taken as complementary to the preceding Book of Justice. It is, as Spenser has presented both Virtues, easier but misleading to take it as a delightful contrast. No Virtue should come as a *relief* from any other. Spenser makes this integral connection clear in his narrative plan. Artegall, returning from suppressing Grantorto, meets Calidore and asks the nature of his quest:

> The Blattant Beast (quoth he) I doe pursew,
> And through the world incessantly doe chase,
> Till I him ouertake, or else subdew;
> Yet know I not or how, or in what place
> To find him out, yet still I forward trace.
> What is that Blattant Beast? (then he replide.)
> It is a Monster bred of hellishe race,
> (Then answered he) which often hath annoyd
> Good Knights and Ladies true, and many else destroyd,
>
> FAERIE QUEENE VI, *1*, 7

And Artegall recalls the Beast that harried him as he left Ireland.

The Book deals very little with the actual quest. Courtesy is a Virtue inherent in the exercise of every noble quality. The whole poem is really one long series of examples of courteous action:

> Of Court it seemes, men Courtesie doe call,
> For that it there most vseth to abound;
> And well beseemeth that in Princes hall
> That vertue should be plentifully found,
> Which of all goodly manners is the ground,
> And roote of ciuill conuersation.
> Right so in Faery court it did redound,
> Where curteous Knights and Ladies most did won
> Of all on earth, and made a matchlesse paragon.
>
> FAERIE QUEENE VI, *1*, I

Aristotle says of good temper, 'A good-tempered or gentle person is inclined to forgiveness rather than revenge', and this is a notable feature of Calidore. He spares Crudor (Cruel Disdain), not out of the same laxity as led Artegall to spare Radigund, but on condition of his amendment of life: one function of Courtesy, then, is reforming Justice.

For one of the Virtues which Aristotle discusses, he can find no name. It 'most nearly resembles friendliness', but 'it differs from friendliness in being destitute of emotion or affection for the people with whom one associates. . . . For he will so act alike to strangers and acquaintances, and to persons with whom he is not intimate . . . he will never lose sight of what is noble and expedient . . . he will render to each class its proper due.' There *is* a word for this Virtue, or at least for its Christian application: Charity or *Agape*. And of this Virtue, Courtesy is the social application:

> What vertue is so fitting for a knight,
> Or for a Ladie, whom a knight should loue,
> As Curtesie, to beare themselues aright
> To all of each degree, as doth behoue?

FAERIE QUEENE VI, 2, 1

In Book VI, Spenser is concerned to exemplify Courtesy and its opposite, and to analyse it: not only its scope and functions but its nature and origins. He says that among the Virtues

> . . . growes not a fayrer flowre,
> Then is the bloosme of comely courtesie,
> Which though it on a lowly stalke doe bowre,
> Yet brancheth forth in braue nobilitie,
> And spreds it selfe through all ciuilitie:

FAERIE QUEENE VI, Prol. 4

He adds later that this Virtue 'Of all goodly manners is the ground'. This is, to Spenser, true in a double sense. Without Courtesy Virtue is limited, even inoperative. But the 'nobilitie' into which Courtesy grows is nobility of blood as well as of mind. Courtesy will find its own level. Conversely, courteous behaviour is natural to those of noble blood, by reason of this origin of nobility. In Book I, Satyrane, who has been brought up 'emongst wild beasts and woods', responds instantly to Una's 'curteous deeds', and

Thenceforth he kept her goodly company,
And learned her discipline of faith and veritie.

FAERIE QUEENE I, 6, 31

Spenser presents a number of variations on the theme of the response of noble blood to the stimulus of noble, that is courteous, action or challenge. Tristram, son of King Meliogras, has been brought up in the forest. He has learnt hunting, hawking and other aristocratic sports, but not the use of arms. But he is moved by the sight of a knight ill-treating a lady to intervene, and to slay the aggressor. By so doing, he has infringed the law of arms, as Calidore points out:

Why hath thy hand too bold it selfe embrewed
In blood of knight, the which by thee is slaine,
By thee no knight; which armes impugneth plaine?

FAERIE QUEENE VI, 2, 7

But he has fulfilled the demands of Courtesy, as Calidore comes to understand. The natural laws of Virtue take precedence over the usages of society when they do not serve their proper function of supporting it. Calidore accordingly grants Tristram's request:

That ye will make me Squire without delay,
That from henceforth in batteilous array
I may beare armes, and learne to vse them right;

FAERIE QUEENE VI, 2, 33

Tristram now has the opportunity of exercising his virtue to the full in the right context of knightly action.

The Salvage Man who rescues Calepine and befriends Serena acts with perfect natural courtesy:

. . . that neuer till this houre
Did taste of pittie, neither gentlesse knew.

FAERIE QUEENE VI, 4, 3

At the beginning of the following canto it is strongly hinted that he is of noble blood:

O what an easie thing is to descry
The gentle bloud, how euer it be wrapt

In sad misfortunes foule deformity,
And wretched sorrowes, which haue often hapt? . . .

That plainely may in this wyld man be red, . . .
For certes he was borne of noble blood,
How euer by hard hap he hether came; . . .

FAERIE QUEENE VI, 5, 1–2

Though the Salvage has never had occasion to exercise the faculties that such noble descent would imply, when he finds himself in a situation to which they are appropriate he responds by instinct, though he cannot clothe his actions with the grace that comes only from noble education.

This whole theme is worked out most fully in the character of Pastorella, who has been brought up in the Valley of the Shepherds. She is recognised as being pre-eminent among the shepherdesses: Calidore's first sight of her shows her naturally superior position:

Vpon a litle hillocke she was placed
Higher than all the rest, and round about
Enuiron'd with a girland, goodly graced,
Of louely lasses, . . .

FAERIE QUEENE VI, 9, 8

Having been brought up by Meliboe, who has spent some time at Court before his retirement to the Valley, she is not untutored in gracious manners. But she is content that they should be appropriate to her situation, as Calidore discovers:

But she that neuer had acquainted beene
With such queint vsage, fit for Queenes and Kings,
Ne euer had such knightly seruice seene,
But being bred vnder base shepheards wings,
Had euer learn'd to loue the lowly things,
Did litle whit regard his courteous guize, . . .

FAERIE QUEENE VI, 9, 35

Calidore in fact has been paying court to her essential nature, which is not yet fully developed, rather than to her as she at present is, and so:

137

> . . . (he) thought it best
> To chaunge the manner of his loftie looke;
> And doffing his bright armes, himselfe addrest
> In shepheards weed, . . .

FAERIE QUEENE VI, *9*, 36

Pastorella's noble character is brought fully to life, not by the sight of courtly manners that are inappropriate to the life she lives, but by the display of the qualities they grace. When she is attacked by a tiger, Coridon, her rustic lover, flees: the virtues of a shepherd do not include knightly courage. Calidore rescues her, and:

> From that day forth she gan him to affect,
> And daily more her fauour to augment;
> But *Coridon* for cowherdize reiect,
> Fit to keepe sheepe, vnfit for loues content:

FAERIE QUEENE VI, *10*, 37

Having once understood noble virtue, she has in a sense out-grown the pastoral world. The catastrophe that takes her from it happens almost at once, and she is quickly brought to her real parents and so to the noble life and its responsibilities.

This is an important point. Courtesy is at once the origin and the sign of nobility. But nobility is, in essence, the desire, linked with the capacity, for *active* virtue. Spenser's Virtues go armed, as knights errant; they do not form a closed circle at the Faerie Court. Rather the Court and its sovereign are a centre from which virtue proceeds, and to which its glory and fame return. So virtue proceeds from Heaven, and the virtuous soul attains heavenly immortality. Spenser addresses the Queen:

> Then pardon me, most dreaded Soueraine,
> That from your selfe I doe this vertue bring,
> And to your selfe doe it returne againe:
> So from the Ocean all riuers spring,
> And tribute backe repay as to their King.

FAERIE QUEENE VI, Prol. 7

Knighthood is the privilege of nobility, because only noble natures are capable of accepting its responsibilities.

In this, as elsewhere in his portrayal of Courtesy, Spenser echoes the thought of his time. In particular he touches on the theme of the decay of Courtesy:

> Of which though present age doe plenteous seeme,
> Yet being matcht with plaine Antiquitie,
> Ye will them all but fayned showes esteeme.

FAERIE QUEENE Prol. 4

All his examples of untutored nobility have their upbringing far from the Court, and this is true of Arthur also (I, 9). For although: 'Of Court it seemes, men Courtesie doe call' (VI, 1, 1) even that perfected Faerie Court which Spenser has deduced imaginatively from the Court of Elizabeth has heard of the Blatant Beast. Its depredations are examined from another angle in *Mother Hvbberds Tale* (p. 46). Calidore's quest leads him through every range of human society:

> Him first from court he to the citties coursed,
> And from the citties to the townes him prest,
> And from the townes into the countrie forsed,
> And from the country back to priuate farmes he scorsed.

FAERIE QUEENE VI, 9, 3

It is only when he inquires of the shepherds that

> They answer'd him, that no such beast they saw, . . .

FAERIE QUEENE VI, 9, 6

It is a paradox of the fallen, even the Faerie world, that it is only in this place remote from all society that Courtesy can be naturally exercised, where it has no active, militant function.

The story of this Book falls into three parts. First we see Calidore on his quest, and his adventures provide examples of Courtesy: his reform of Crudor and Briana, his meeting with Tristram and his protection of Priscilla's good fame. His rescue of Serena from the Blatant Beast, which initiates the second part of the Book, is a deliberate parallel to this last episode, for the Blatant Beast is every kind of slander and ill-will, and Serena, being a woman, is particularly vulnerable. Calidore's pursuit of the Beast now takes him out of the action. There follow the adventures of Serena and Calepine, her knight, their separation and misfortunes, and Arthur is introduced as Serena's protector, taking her to a hermit, who cures her rankling wounds. He himself goes on to encounter Mirabella. She has sinned against Courtesy by treating her lovers cruelly, and Cupid had condemned her to ride in penance on an ass, belaboured by Disdaine, and weeping bitterly, until she has saved as many lovers as she herself has slain. Here again the operations of Courtesy are shown as intimately linked with those of Justice. The whole allegorical form of this passage is very strongly reminiscent of the medieval allegorical romances of courtly love: Mirabella's sin has been less against Love than against the exercise of charity within its social conventions.

The discursive form of this part of the narrative displays the varied manifestations of Courtesy and also the terrible forces that oppose it. The climax is Calepine's rescue of Serena from the Cannibals, whose lascivious barbarity is the complement to the destructive cruelty of the Beast. These savages are corrupt in mind as in manners; they instinctively see all that is fair in a degrading light. In this they typify the gloating satisfaction of the base and unclean-minded at the misfortunes of those more noble than themselves. The vivid physicality with which this is presented is sickening:

> Now being naked, to their sordid eyes
> The goodly threasures of nature appeare:
> Which as they view with lustfull fantasyes,
> Each wisheth to him selfe, and to the rest enuyes.

FAERIE QUEENE VI, *8*, 41

The third and last part of the Book is centred on the Valley of the Shepherds. Here Calidore takes refreshment. But it is Pastorella for whom he puts off his armour, and for whom he lengthens his stay. In this delay he is at fault, though true love is natural to the full completion of the Virtue he patronises, and Spenser says he is not to be greatly blamed. In the Valley Courtesy informs everyday living, simply and naturally, and it is here that Calidore sees the Vision of the Graces, whose Dance is the visible manifestation of Courtesy in its gracious order:

An hundred naked maidens lilly white,
All raunged in a ring, and dauncing in delight.

FAERIE QUEENE VI, *10*, II

They dance about the Three, to whom is added a Fourth:
Rosalind, the beloved of Colin, to whose music they dance.
Colin is Spenser's own name for himself since *The Shepheardes
Calender*. He is the Poet, in whom virtue is properly contem-
plative rather than active. He can see it as in this vision, as it
divinely is. And by seeing it in his beloved, he can raise her,
through his vision, to its higher reality. Calidore is privileged to
glimpse the vision:

But soone as he appeared to their vew,
They vanisht all away out of his sight, . . .

FAERIE QUEENE VI, *10*, 18

He is a lover; it is this rather than his virtue which allows him
just to see the Graces. But his proper sphere is that of action. It is
not his part to gaze on the Graces, any more than he should
devote his life to the service of Pastorella, whose beauty is
derived from theirs. He should rather implement their power in
the world. Soon, when Calidore is absent hunting, brigands
come and destroy the Valley and steal Pastorella. In the Valley of
the Shepherds, Courtesy flourishes, but its peace and beauty are,
in a fallen world, defenceless. That is why Virtue should not
retire there. Such rest as Calidore has enjoyed is not corrupting:
it is nothing like Verdant's bondage in Acrasia's Bower. But
knightly virtue carries with it war-like responsibility to defend
the good against the ever threatening forces of evil. So Calidore
is recalled to the world of action. He arms himself again, and
pursues the brigands, rescuing Pastorella. He then takes her to
the Castle of Bellamour and Claribell, her true parents. In this
situation of noble reconciliation, Calidore remembers his quest.
Leaving his beloved in her rightful home, he again follows the
Beast, and at last finds it, destroying churches (see p. 36). He
overcomes it, and muzzling it, leads it in triumph through
Faerie Land.

But—the Blatant Beast is not killed. Slander and evil-mindedness can be restrained, but not destroyed, and even such restraint will only be temporary:

> Vntill that, whether wicked fate so framed,
> Or fault of men, he broke his yron chaine,
> And got into the world at liberty againe.

FAERIE QUEENE VI, 12, 38

THE 'MUTABILITIE CANTOS'

The *Mutabilitie Cantos* first appeared in the 1609 Folio of *The Faerie Queene*, with this title: *Two Cantos of Mutabilitie: Which, both for Forme and Matter, appeare to be parcell of some following Booke of the Faerie Queene, Vnder the Legend of Constancie. Neuer before imprinted.* They are numbered six and seven and are followed by two verses, as of an eighth.

From their form and from this description, it is usually assumed that they were part of the uncompleted *Faerie Queene*; and I myself believe this. But it has been pointed out that so long an allegorical passage, without mention of any of the characters of the narrative, would be unparalleled in *The Faerie Queene* as we have it. The *Cantos* may therefore be a separate and complete poem.

The subject, Mutabilitie's challenge to the Gods, and the resolution of this debate and definition of her power by Nature is as was seen at the end of Chapter 3, the culmination of Spenser's lifelong fascination with the whole theme of transience. It is also his last word on the subject, and is perhaps his greatest poetical achievement.

Canto 6 opens with a verse lamenting the effects of Mutabilitie:

> What man that sees the euer-whirling wheele
> Of *Change*, the which all mortall things doth sway,
> But that therby doth find, and plainly feele,
> How MVTABILITY in them doth play
> Her cruell sports, to many mens decay?

MUTABILITIE 6, I

—and Spenser adds that he will tell how she attempted to take away the empire of the Gods, so that her power 'may better yet appear': that is, be made clear by being seen in a universal context.

He goes on to give the lineage of Mutabilitie. She is:

> ... a daughter by descent
> Of those old *Titans*, that did whylome striue
> With *Saturnes* sonne for heauens regiment.
> Whom, though high *Ioue* of kingdome did depriue,
> Yet many of their stemme long after did suruiue.

MUTABILITIE 6, 2

Jove here stands for God: the Titans are the rebel angels, who fell from Heaven, but who still, as devils, have the power God permits them.

Mutabilitie therefore is a result of the Fall. She seeks to pervert the original order of the created world:

> And all the worlds faire frame (which none yet durst
> Of Gods or men to alter or misguide)
> She alter'd quite, and made them all accurst
> That God had blest;

MUTABILITIE 6, 5

Not only in the natural world, but in all social and legal order, her power is felt, with cumulative effects: a deepening process of decay, which is a central idea in Spenser's work:

> And all this world is woxen daily worse.
> O pittious worke of MVTABILITIE!
> By which, we all are subiect to that curse,
> And death in stead of life haue sucked from our Nurse.

MUTABILITIE 6, 6

The full force of this image can be seen if it is compared with all the images of fertility, physical and spiritual, which Spenser uses elsewhere to express the nature and activity of virtue and beauty: in particular the figure of Charity and her babes (*Faerie Queene*, I, *10*, 30–1) of which this is a horrifying reversal (see the illustration opposite p. 88).

From the earth, Mutabilitie ascends through the elements of

air and fire that lie between the earth and the sphere of the Moon. (It was generally held that the corruption of the Fall extended up to the Moon, the inmost of the heavenly spheres.) The Moon is incorrupt in itself. It is 'made of the heauens substance', that is, of the quintessence, the fifth element, which being a perfect mixture is not subject to decay, as John Donne says, in *The Good Morrow*: 'What ever dies was not mixed equally'.

Her struggle with the Goddess of the Moon causes an eclipse, and the Gods rush to Jove in terror. It is clear from the description of Mercury, 'that next doth raigne', and '*Ioues* faire Palace, fixt in heauens hight' (*Mutabilitie 6*, 14–15) that the Gods here are the planets, who moderate human destiny, by their influence over the earth. This influence is in its nature good, as they are incorrupt, though since the world is fallen it may have evil effects. But they are not omnipotent: they represent the planetary Intelligences, the angels set to watch over each planet in its sphere. Mercury is sent to the Moon to discover:

> . . . if that any were on earth belowe
> That did with charmes or Magick her molest,
> Him to attache, and down to hell to throwe:
> But, if from heauen it were, then to arrest
> The Author.

MUTABILITIE 6, 16

This refers to the magical feat (for which charms exist from classical times onwards) of bringing down the Moon from Heaven. Mercury finds Mutabilitie, and treats her as being 'of heaven', a spiritual, not an earthly being. He tries the power of his rod (which is the power of concord as exemplified in the movements of the heavenly bodies and their influence), of the same wood as the Palmer's staff (*Faerie Queene* II, *12*, 41) and of the same form as Cambina's rod of peace (*Faerie Queene* IV, *3*, 42); but in vain. Mutabilitie implies discord, rebellion against authority:

> Ne shee the lawes of Nature onely brake,
> But eke of Iustice, and of Policie;

MUTABILITIE 6, 6

Jove, hearing of this, recalls the rebellion of the Titans, and calls the other divinities to consider how best to restrain this new threat: 'Areed ye sonnes of God, as best ye can deuise' (*Mutabilitie 6*, 21); which makes it clear that his authority, though divine, is derived from God Himself, and is manifest, like that of the other planets, in the created universe. This may be compared to the concept of the Graces, who are derived from Venus, and whose powers are seen in lovely human behaviour.

Mutabilitie now ascends of her own free will to the planetary sphere of Jove himself, and challenges his sovereignty. His arguments are of no avail:

> ... we by Conquest of our soueraine might,
> And by eternall doome of Fates decree,
> Haue wonne the Empire of the Heauens bright.

MUTABILITIE *6*, 33

These are the physical heavens: the spheres of the planets and the fixed stars. He bids her:

> ... seeke by grace and goodnesse to obtaine
> That place from which by folly *Titan* fell.

MUTABILITIE *6*, 34

Spenser may here be recalling Lucifer's title, 'Son of the Morning', sometimes taken to refer to the Morning Star:

> How art thou fallen from heaven, Lucifer, Son of the Morning. . . .
> For thou hast said in thine heart I will ascend unto heaven, I will exalt my throne above the Stars of God.

ISAIAH *14*, 12–13

But Mutabilitie appeals to God Himself:

> But to the highest him, that is behight
> Father of Gods and men by equall might;
> To weet, the God of Nature, I appeale.

MUTABILITIE *6*, 35

With this challenge, the first section of the allegory closes. There follows an interlude, where, though the effects of Mutabilitie are demonstrated, they are expressed in a less elevated vein.

The place chosen for the trial of Mutabilitie's cause is Arlo, in

Ireland. For this there are two probable reasons. First, Spenser wished to fit the application of his great allegory firmly into the context of his own world. Secondly, he loved the country of Ireland, though he hated its rebellious inhabitants: by choosing this setting he had the opportunity to celebrate the beauties of the one, and deplore the wretchedness caused by the viciousness of the other.

The purpose of this interlude that precedes the judgement is to:

> . . . tell how *Arlo* through *Dianaes* spights
> (Beeing of old the best and fairest Hill
> That was in all this holy-Islands hights)
> Was made the most vnpleasant, and most ill.

MUTABILITIE 6, 37

The change of style from epic to pastoral is quite deliberate, and Spenser offers an apology:

> And, were it not ill fitting for this file,
> To sing of hilles and woods, mongst warres and Knights,
> I would abate the sterneness of my stile,
> Mongst these sterne stounds to mingle soft delights.

MUTABILITIE 6, 37

Then follows the tale of the river nymph Molanna, (this passage is reminiscent of the great marriage feast of the Rivers which is the climax to Book IV) an attendant of Diana who loved to hunt in the woods round Arlo. The foolish satyr, Faunus, longed to see Diana bathing, and won Molanna to help him to this end:

> So, her with flattering words he first assaid;
> And after, pleasing gifts for her purvaid,
> Queene-apples, and red Cherries from the tree.

MUTABILITIE 6, 43

Molanna agrees on condition that Faunus will undertake to help her win the river Fanchin for her love; the use of this theme here is interesting. This love is not a glorious, public marriage of the elements as in Book IV, but secret, and evil comes of its hopes. For Faunus, seeing Diana naked, laughs for joy:

> . . . A foolish *Faune* indeed,
> That couldst not hold thy selfe so hidden blest.

MUTABILITIE 6, 46

Enraged, the Goddess and her maidens set upon him and torment him, and at last hunt him with their hounds. The episode is reminiscent of Actaeon who also saw Diana naked, but he was transformed to a deer and killed by his own hounds. Here Diana is more merciful, and the Faun is allowed to escape. Molanna they overwhelm with stones, but Faunus keeps his promise:

> So now her waues passe through a pleasant Plaine,
> Till with the *Fanchin* she herselfe doe wed,
> And (both combin'd) them selues in one faire riuer spred.

MUTABILITIE 6, 53

The outcome is not tragic, and the whole episode, with Diana's rough justice, provides a kind of antimasque to the solemn judgement to be given in the next canto. But Diana from that time has forsaken Ireland, and wolves and thieves abound there to this day. 'Which too-too true that lands in-dwellers since haue found' (6, 55).

Canto 7 deals with the judgement itself. Spenser invokes the Divine Muse:

> . . . in my feeble brest
> Kindle fresh sparks of that immortall fire,
> Which learned minds inflameth with desire
> Of heauenly things:

MUTABILITIE 7, 2

At Arlo Hill all the Gods assemble, all the powers of the planets and of the elements:

> As well those that are sprung of heauenly seed,
> As those that all the other world doe fill,
> And rule both sea and land vnto their will:

MUTABILITIE 7, 3

and all other living creatures. They are set in their right places by Order, 'Nature's Sergeant'.

Then Nature comes: Nature as the creative power of God Him-self: His vice-regent in all that He has made. She is greater than any of the Gods, and she is veiled:

> That some doe say was so by skill deuized,
> To hide the terror of her vncouth hew,
> From mortall eyes that should be sore agrized;
> For that her face did like a Lion shew,
> That eye of wight could not indure to view:
> But others tell that it so beautious was,
> And round about such beames of splendor threw,
> That it the Sunne a thousand times did pass,
> Ne could be seene, but like an image in a glass.

MUTABILITIE 7, 6

Nature's beauty is Divinity itself. It can only be seen in the creation, diffused into form, 'like an image in a glass'. Her glory is compared to that of Christ Himself at the Transfiguration, and as God's creative power she *is* in one sense Christ: the Second Person of the Trinity whom St. John calls the Logos, the Word of God:

> In the beginning was the Word, and the Word was with God, and the Word was God. The same was in the beginning with God. All things were made by him, and without him was not anything made that was made.

JOHN 1, 1–3

And before this terrifyingly glorious being all the world rejoices; flowers bloom, the rivers run freshly and:

> Was neuer so great ioyance since the day,
> That all the gods whylome assembled were,
> On *Haemus* hill in their diuine array,
> To celebrate the solemne bridall cheare,
> Twixt *Peleus*, and dame *Thetis* pointed there;

MUTABILITIE 7, 12

The whole creation is assembled to hear a final judgement on itself, for Mutabilitie's ambition affects all things. The occasion is solemn beyond imagination: the Judge supreme. And in her presence all rejoice as at a wedding. This is the culmination of all Spenser's great images of marriage and fertility to express joy and virtue and beauty. It is indeed, hardly an image at all. It is the thing itself. In the judgement of Nature we see, directly, the nature of God Himself.

Mutabilitie says:

> For, heauen and earth I both alike do deeme,
> Sith heauen and earth are both alike to thee;

MUTABILITIE 7, 15

(But Mutabilitie is not Nature. Mutabilitie is confusing absence of respect for different degrees with impartial justice over them.) She then adds the justification of her claim. All things on earth grow and die. Winter succeeds spring. Good fortune is followed by bad. The elements are all unstable, subject to tide, or wind, heat or cold—and they are the very foundation of matter.

Nature allows her to call her witnesses, who follow, in procession. First the Seasons, and the Months, each accompanied by the Zodiacal sign belonging to it, appear with their traditional attributes: you may see them in the misericord carvings in Malvern Priory, and elsewhere. Spenser may, as in the case of the Seven Deadly Sins (p. 97) have specific tapestries or pictures in mind. All are in themselves fair, or gay, or sad according to the time of the year. Then follow Day and Night, and the Hours, and at last Life and Death. Mutabilitie appeals:

> Lo, mighty mother, now be iudge and say,
> Whether in all thy creatures more or lesse
> CHANGE doth not raign and beare the greatest sway:

MUTABILITIE 7, 47

To this Jove has to agree.

Mutabilitie goes on to challenge the planetary Gods: the changes of the Moon, the variations of Mercury and Venus, the erratic orbit of Mars, the differing aspects of Saturn, and of Jove himself. Even if the legends of his birth on earth are false or inapplicable, the influence of his planet changes:

> . . . from his nature trew,
> By others opposition or obliquid view.

MUTABILITIE 7, 54

that is, by the varying conjunctions. So since:

> . . . within this wide great Vniuerse
> Nothing doth firme and permanent appeare,
> But all things tost and turned by transuerse:
> What then should let, but I aloft should reare
> My Trophee, and from all, the triumph beare?

MUTABILITIE 7, 56

To this Nature replies that change is inherent in creation only because it is through growth in time that each being attains eternal stability.

There remain two verses: the eighth canto, *Vnperfite*. These bring Nature's words down from the divine to the human view point.

> When I bethinke me on that speech whyleare,
> Of *Mutability*, and well it way:
> Me seemes, that though she all vnworthy were
> Of the Heav'ns Rule; yet very sooth to say,
> In all things else she beares the greatest sway.

But the judgement of Nature is of the very essence of right hope, of informed desire for the Divine, the good, the beautiful:

> For, all that moueth, doth in *Change* delight:
> But thence-forth all shall rest eternally
> With Him that is the God of Sabbaoth hight:
> O that great Sabbaoth God, graunt me that Sabaoths sight.

Though *The Faerie Queene* remains unfinished, we have here the conclusive statement of its full meaning.

5

Spenser's Other Poems

Spenser's other writings have been frequently referred to already, particularly in Chapter 2. Here I shall consider, in order of publication, the most important of these poems in their own right, especially as indicating the use made by Spenser of different conventions.

'THE SHEPHEARDES CALENDER'

'THE SHEPHEARDES CALENDER'

Spenser's first original work was published in 1579 and was much praised. Sir Philip Sidney, to whom it was dedicated, commends in *An Apologie for Poetrie* (1583) 'the much poetrie in the *Eclogues*', although he felt that he 'could not allow that same framing of his style in an old and rustic language'. Thomas Nashe, on the other hand, acclaims Spenser as 'the miracle of art, line for line for my life in the honor of England against Spaine, France, Italie, and all the world' (Preface to *Menaphon*, 1589). The playwright, George Peele, takes the names of some of Spenser's shepherds for the pastoral scenes in his *Arraignment of Paris*, acted in 1580, thus paying Spenser the compliment of regarding his work as delightfully fashionable: the *Arraignment* is a highly sophisticated piece intended for court entertainment.

Spenser published the *Calender* under the name of *Immerito*, which he uses also in his correspondence with Gabriel Hervey. The introductory epistle to Hervey which prefaces the *Calender*, together with an 'argument of the whole booke' and notes to the individual eclogues, were contributed by E.K., probably Edward Kirke, a contemporary of Spenser's at Pembroke Hall. Before examining the *Eclogues* themselves as they stand in the light of E.K.'s editorship, it should be pointed out that E.K.'s ignorance as to the meaning of various passages and allusions is almost certainly assumed. It seems very likely that E.K.'s 'elucidations' had Spenser's full knowledge and approval, and that the veil of mystery which he casts over various passages is calculated. In a case such as that of Dido, whose death is lamented in the *November Eclogue*, this secrecy may perhaps be a matter of fact, although when E.K. says: 'The personage is secrete, and to me altogether vnknowne, albe of him selfe I often required the same', he is probably being rather disingenuous. But in the various notes on Hobbinol (Gabriel Hervey), as to whose identity E.K. feigns ignorance when commenting on the *January Eclogue*, only to reveal it in a note to the *September Eclogue*, it is clear that the mystery is part of a private literary joke, the significance of which would be clear to all members of Spenser's own circle, among whom the *Eclogues* would certainly have been circulated before publication. The portentous solemnity of E.K.'s apology for his editorship has the same ring.

The Shepheardes Calender is Spenser's apprentice-work in the classical pattern laid out by the work of Virgil particularly. In his Epistle, and again in the Argument, E.K. is seriously concerned to make this clear.

E.K.'s two other principal concerns are the form and style of the work. The plan is original. Spenser has written twelve eclogues, one for each month of the year, and has given them the title of *The Shepheardes Calender*, 'an old title' taken from the French *Kalendrier des Bergers*, the English translation of which was well known. This was a kind of handbook almanac, comprising popular science and devotion (Roman Catholic) illustrated by woodcuts. Spenser may have had some idea of counteracting its influence by his own Protestant doctrine, but the plan is quite different. Spenser's twelve eclogues are written in varying modes, as will be seen, but the whole plan, from January to December (he is using the agricultural year, not that of the calendar of his day, which began the year in March, as in the procession of the Months in *Mutabilitie 7*), is intended to reflect the course of human life from youth to age, and also the course of human love, of which the pastoral is the proper poetic expression, from youthful passion to that maturity of experience from which the poet may hope to leave these lighter, personal matters for the more serious work of epic. It is probable that the suggestion for such a plan came from Marot's *Eclogue du Roy*, which developed a comparison between the course of human life and the changing seasons, and which Spenser uses as a source for his *December Eclogue*.

In discussing the style of the poem, E.K. anticipated such criticism as Sidney's of the use of rustic, even dialect words. But this he presents as a merit:

> For in my opinion it is one special prayse of many whych are dew to this Poete, that he hath laboured to restore, as to their rightfull heritage such good and naturall English words, as haue ben long time out of vse and almost cleane disherited. Which is the onely cause, that our Mother tonge, which truely of it self is both ful enough for prose and stately enough for verse, hath long time ben counted most bare and barrein of both.

Spenser's use of archaisms is intended to draw on the wealth and the literary associations of his English predecessors. In glossing the 'strange' words used by Spenser, E.K. refers them to Chaucer or Lydgate whenever possible. This indicates both patriotic pride and reverence for his earlier models, and it is his constant method. In the spelling and vocabulary of *The Faerie Queene* there is certainly nothing deliberately rustic: that would be unsuitable in an epic, but his constant use of archaic words and forms to develop his own style to suit his complex purpose is comparable to Milton's heavily Latinate style, which is meant to recall, by its very form and syntax, Virgil, his great model.

The *Eclogues* themselves, E.K. says in the Argument:

> may well be diuided into three formes orranckes. For eyther they be Plaintive, . . . or recreative such as al those be, which conceiue matter of loue, or commendation of special personages, or Moral: which for the most part he mixed with some Satyrical bitternesse. . . .

The *January Eclogue* comes under E.K.'s heading of plaintive. Colin Cloute, who is Spenser himself (he appears again, piping to the Dance of the Graces, *Faerie Queene* VI, *10*), compares his grief in love to the season of the year:

> Thou barrein ground, whome winters wrath hath wasted,
> Art made a myrrhour, to behold my plight:

18–19

This poem appears both simple and delightful, but in the context of the *Calender* it outlines the plan of the whole.

The *February Eclogue* is moral: 'of reverence due to old age'. But the tale, a moral fable like those of Aesop, of the briar's scorn for the oak-tree whose protection she sorely missed when it was cut down, is not only an apt rebuke to the impertinent Cuddie, but is a moral emblem of the state of the world, and the fate of unwise ambition. Thenot's first reply to Cuddie's discontent shows that the situation of the eclogue should be applied in a wider context than that of age and youthful folly; it anticipates Nature's great judgement at the end of the *Mutabilitie Cantos*, showing that age and experience can achieve a right perspective, though one limited here to the moral level:

> Must not the world wend in his commun course
> From good to badd and from badde to worse,
> From worse vnto that is worst of all,
> And then returne to his former fall?

11–14

The *March Eclogue* deals with love, and so is recreative: 'to springtime is most agreeable'. The theme, of the hunting of Cupid, is a traditional one; but the Mediterranean origins of this Cupid show rather startlingly in an English spring:

> With that sprong forth a naked swayne,
> With spotted winges like Peacocks trayne,
>   And laughing lope to a tree.
> His gylden quiuer at his backe,
> And siluer bowe, which was but slacke,
>   Which lightly he bent at me.

79–84

This poem treats of love lightly and wittily, but the subject itself is serious. The pains of youthful passion may pass, may be scorned from the standpoint of mature experience, but they are real and agonising enough. Thomalin is struck by a dart:

For then I little smart did feele:
　　But soone it sore encreased.
And now itranckleth more and more,
And inwardly it festreth sore,
　　Ne wote I, how to cease it.

98–102

This image of corruption and disease should be compared with the description of Cupid's power as this is displayed in the House of Busyrane (*Faerie Queene* IV, *12*).

The *April Eclogue* is also recreative, being one of those which deal with 'commendation of special personages', in this case Queen Elizabeth. The framework of Colin's *Songe* in her honour is the discussion between Thenot and Hobbinol of his unhappy love, so that the main plan of the poem is touched on and emphasised. The song itself is the first example in Spenser's work of his extraordinary genius for inventing verse forms. The famous flower verse may be quoted as an example of the lovely and delicate effect he has here achieved:

Bring hether the Pincke and purple Cullambine,
　　With Gelliflowres:
Bring Coronations, and Sops in wine,
　　worne of Paramoures.
Strowe me the ground with Daffadowndillies,
And Cowslips, and Kingcups, and loued Lillies:
　　The pretie Pawnce,
　　And the Cheuisaunce,
Shall match with the fayre flowre Delice.

136–44

(The *Chevisaunce* is almost certainly a printer's misreading of *Cherisance*—a clove-scented pink.) It is possible that Milton had this passage in mind when he wrote the flower passage in *Lycidas*.

The *May Eclogue* is a moral eclogue 'of coloured deceipt': the first in which Spenser uses the possibilities of the pastoral for ecclesiastical allegory, by a play on the word *pastor*, meaning shepherd and priest. It is a dispute between a Catholic and a Protestant priest, and the moral fable, reminiscent in form of

Thenot's tale in the *February Eclogue*, is directed against the deceits of the Roman Church (the Fox), disguised as a pedlar, who traps the Kid by showing him his gaudy wares. The implication is that the Kid (not a lamb but a young goat) is damned as a result of his folly (see pp. 37–8).

The *June Eclogue* is again plaintive. Colin bewails the unsuccessful course of his love for Rosalind, and this season of middle summer is appropriate to increasing maturity:

> And I, whylst youth, and course of carelesse yeeres
> Did let me walke withouten lincks of loue,
> In such delights did ioy amongst my peeres:
> But ryper age such pleasures doth reproue.

33–6

Hobbinol (Hervey) attempts to encourage Colin's poetic ambitions, but the time for this is not yet:

> I neuer lyst presume to *Parnasse* hyll,
> Buy pyping lowe in shade of lowly groue,
> I play to please my selfe, all be it ill.

70–2

The *Eclogue* then takes in another theme of the whole *Calender*: the decline of poetry in England (see pp. 11, 44 sqq.).

The *July Eclogue* is again moral 'of dissolute shepheards and pastours': the theme is pride and ambition in the priesthood. Morrell, who sits upon a hill, represents these vices; Tomalin, who finds that 'In humble dales is footing fast' (13), is a 'good shephearde', a humble and conscientious priest, as opposed to Morrell who is, significantly, a goatherd.

The *August Eclogue* is recreative. It takes the form of a poetic contest between two shepherds and, as E.K. points out, Spenser has used Theocritus and Virgil as models. At the close of the roundel (of which they sing alternate lines), Cuddie, the judge, recites 'a proper song, whereof Colin sayth he was Authour', lamenting his grief for Rosalind, and vowing to live a solitary life till death:

> . . . Here will I dwell apart
> In gastfull groue therefore, till my laste sleepe

169–70

—or until she returns to him.

The *September Eclogue* is again moral and, like the *July Eclogue*, 'of dissolute shepheards and pastours'. The theme here is of Diggon's return from a hopeful journey abroad. His flock is lost and wasted, and he is bitterly disillusioned with the state of the Roman Church as he has found it to be:

> For eyther the shepeheards bene ydle and still,
> And ledde of theyr sheepe, what way they wyll:
> Or they bene false, and full of couetise,
> And casten to compasse many wrong emprise.

80–3

This theme, of the scandal of Catholic abuses, is elaborated, and applied to the Church of England, which despite the Reformation is still not free from corruption:

> But the fewer Woolues (the soth to sayne,)
> The more bene the Foxes that here remaine.

154–5

This theme is elaborated more fully in the character of the 'formall priest' in *Mother Hvbberds Tale*.

The *October Eclogue* is also moral, and deals with 'the contempt of Poetrie and pleasant wits', picking up the theme from the second part of the *June Eclogue*. Here Cuddie, who was judge of the contest in the *July Eclogue*, 'is set out the perfecte paterne of a Poete, whiche finding no maintenaunce of his state and studies, complayneth of the contempte of Poetrie, and the causes thereof'. Although Spenser does not use his own *persona* here of Colin, it is clearly his own ambitions and opinions which are meant. Probably he did not wish to offend such friends as Sidney by seeming to apply his comments too particularly to his own situation. But Pierce urges Cuddie to aspire to the writing of epic, as Hobbinol did Colin in the *June Eclogue*, and it is clear that Spenser has *The Faerie Queene* in mind:

157

> Whither thou list in fayre *Elisa* rest,
> Or if thee please in bigger notes to sing,
> Aduaunce the worthy whome shee loueth best.

45–7

Cuddie's response is to bewail the decaying state of patronage, and of that virtue which is the proper subject of verse: this passage was discussed on pages 10–11. A poet must be provided with the necessities of life so that he may pursue his great task undistracted:

> Ne wont with crabbed care the Muses dwell.
> Vnwisely weaues, that takes two webbes in hand.

101–2

The relevance of this to Spenser's own desire for advancement (see pp. 44–7) is clear.

The *November Eclogue* is presumably, from what he says, one whose special purpose and meaning is unknown to E.K. As an elegy it is not strictly recreative, but neither, as dealing with a 'special personage', is it plaintive. This elegy is proper to the time of winter for it deals with death, the end of life's progress: '*Thenot*, now nis the time of merimake' (9). It is another example of Spenser's inventiveness in verse form: marvellously rich and orchestrated in the opportunities it gives for effects of rhyme and assonance.

The *December Eclogue* is again plaintive. It sums up all that has gone before, as Colin compares the course of his life, from youth to age, to the course of the year. And not his life only, as far as the whole plan of the *Calender* is concerned, for the lament is to be applied universally to all, human desire, ambition and mortality. It is a moral perspective in which every human concern which has been touched on can be seen in the light of transience:

> Winter is come, that blowes the balefull breath,
> And after Winter commeth timely death.

149–50

'COMPLAINTS'

The volume entitled *Complaints. Containing sundrie small Poems of the Worlds Vanitie* appeared in 1591, when Spenser's reputation had been strongly established by the appearance of the first three Books of *The Faerie Queene*. Just as Spenser left the presentation of *The Shepheardes Calender* to E.K., so here he would seem to be sheltering behind his publisher, William Ponsonby, who says that the success of *The Faerie Queene* has led him to get all he can of Spenser's other writing into his hands.

It seems likely that Spenser was in part responsible both for the selection of the contents of the volume and their arrangement, and that his apparent casualness served a two-fold purpose. First, it preserved the convention of unconcern with the mere *publication* of poetry: the appeal to a general audience. Secondly, it provided him with some safeguard against the reactions of the authorities to the satirical import of its contents.

The poems in *Complaints* have a striking uniformity of subject-matter. They are elaborate treatments of the main themes of *The Shepheardes Calender*: the decay of the world and of greatness, the fate waiting alike upon aspiring virtue and on careless pride, and the corruption of contemporary society as seen in Church and State. They are variations on the theme of transience and mutability, and show not only Spenser's engrossing interest in the subject; they also appeal to the contemporary taste for melancholy moralisation, which had developed its own literary conventions from the time of Boccaccio and Chaucer onwards.

'THE RUINES OF TIME'

This poem falls into four main divisions: a patriotic lament by the Genius of Verlame (St. Albans) for her past glories; a lament for the great dead of the Leicester and Bedford families; a celebration of the power of poetry to confer lasting fame; and a complaint of the world's vanity. The structure of the poem is, however, so loose that it is possible to believe, like Renwick,[*] that it is made up of fragments originally intended for other

---

[*] W. L. Renwick: *Edmund Spenser* (E. Arnold, 1925).

purposes; he suggests that Spenser has here combined a poem in honour of Camden's *Britannia*, an elegy on Sidney, and parts of the lost *Dreames* or *Pageants*.

In this poem, Spenser—imaginatively excited by antiquarian research, which fits with his own attitude towards the past as a source of inspiration—pays tribute to Camden, one of the most learned of English Renaissance antiquaries:

> *Cambden* the nourice of antiquitie,
> And lanterne vnto late succeeding age,
> To see the light of simple veritie,
> Buried in ruines, through the great outrage
> Of her owne people, led with warlike rage.
> *Cambden*, though time all moniments obscure,
> Yet thy iust labours euer shall endure.

169–75

'THE TEARES OF THE MUSES'

Here Spenser is the spokesman of the new poetry for the literary ideals which he shared with Sidney and his circle. It treats fully the subject of the *October Eclogue*: the state of poetry in England. It opens with an invocation to the Muses:

> Rehearse to me ye sacred Sisters nine,
> The golden brood of great *Apolloes* wit,
> Those piteous plaints. . . .

1–3

and each Muse has a lament, citing her special causes of grievance, and implying the remedy.

'VIRGILS GNAT'

This poem is an adaptation rather than a translation, of the Virgilian *Culex*. Whether or not he wrote it with an allegorical purpose in mind, the dedicatory sonnet to Leicester indicates that it is to be applied in such a way; Spenser is clearly the Gnat, who is punished by the shepherd, Leicester, for warning him against some danger; but *what* danger remains unknown, though there have been varied conjectures.

The Virgilian poem belongs to that *genre* well-established and developed in writing of the classical period, the point of which is made by exaggerating the significance of the essentially trivial. The point of this can be mere charm or prettiness or, as here, it can have a more profound kind of wit: Spenser is the first writer in English to use it as a definite form of satire. *Virgil's Gnat* and *Muiopotmos* are both examples of mock-heroic, of which the greatest practitioners are Dryden and Pope. This appears particularly in the passages of description, in which Spenser elaborates on his original, as here, in the Gnat's Lament with its delightfully inappropriate epic solemnity:

> I carried am into waste wildernesse,
> Waste wildernes, amongst *Cymerian* shades,
> Where endles paines and hideous heauinesse
> Is round about me heapt in darksome glades.

369–72

'MOTHER HUBBERDS TALE'

This is the most direct and powerful of Spenser's satirical works. The passages quoted and discussed in Chapter 2 clearly show how deeply Spenser felt the issues of which he wrote.

The poem is a beast-fable. Spenser is influenced by *Reynard the Fox*, possibly in Caxton's very popular translation. As a satirical method the beast-fable derives from Aesop through many medieval examples, notably Chaucer's *The Nonnes Preestes Tale*.

Spenser sets his tale in a framework. He opens with an adaptation of the traditional 'May Morning' setting for a romance. Spenser's astrological setting is important:

> It was the month, in which the righteous Maide,
> That for disdaine of sinfull worlds vpbraide,
> Fled back to heauen, whence she was first conceiued,
> Into her siluer bowre the Sunne receiued;
> And the hot *Syrian* Dog on him awayting,
> After the chased Lyons cruell bayting,
> Corrupted had th'ayre with his noysome breath,
> And powr'd on th'earth plague, pestilence, and death.

1–8

The maid is Astraea, Goddess of Justice, the instructress of Artegall (*Faerie Queene* V, *1*). She is the Zodiacal sign Virgo. The mention of the other heavenly influences, in particular the reference to plague, has been used in various attempts to date the poem, but whether or not Spenser had a particular outbreak of the plague in mind, he certainly intends that the astrological setting should indicate a state of disorder in society—of which plague was traditionally a cosmic accompaniment and, indeed, result. So Ulysses says in Shakespeare's *Troilus and Cressida*:

> . . . but when the planets
> In evil mixture to disorder wander,
> What plagues and what portents, what mutiny,
> What raging of the sea, shaking of earth,
> Commotion in the winds, fights, changes, horrors,
> Divert and crack, rend and deracinate
> The unity and married calm of state
> Quite from their fixture!

TROILUS AND CRESSIDA I, 3, 94–101

As in Boccaccio's *Decameron*, a group of companions, keeping remote from the plague, beguile the time with stories. Among them is Mother Hubberd who, as her name implies, is no courtly lady. This *persona* is analogous to the rustic shepherds of the *Calender*; she speaks with unsophisticated sincerity, and the style fits both speaker and matter: 'Base is the style, and matter meane withall' (44).

The story of the Ape and his companion, the Fox, has been interpreted as referring to the whole situation of the Queen's proposed marriage with the Duc d'Alençon. This is very probable, but the poem is intended to have a general as well as a topical interpretation. The Fox sums up the philosophy of the wicked pair:

> . . . sith then we are free borne,
> Let vs all seruile base subiection scorne:
> And as we bee sonnes of the world so wide,
> Let vs our fathers heritage diuide.

133–6

This is the logical conclusion of the Giant's arguments for equality confuted by Artegall (*Faerie Queene*, V, 1, see p. 84).

The Fox and the Ape take employment with a shepherd, whose flocks they kill. Being discovered, they enter the Church in response to the advice of the 'formal priest'. On being driven out by their parishioners they meet the vain and foolish Mule (standing for the proud and unworthy courtier), who advises them to go to Court, where they take full advantage of its corrupt state. Eventually they are exposed, and from here the technique of the allegory changes. Up to this point, the force of the satire has been largely derived from the fact that these vicious creatures pass unsuspected among mankind. But now the range and method of the allegory shifts, for they find the Lion, rightful king of beasts (true royalty), sleeping; and stealing his skin, his crown and sceptre (the outward appearance of authority and power), set themselves up in his stead: the Ape as king, the Fox as counsellor. The results of their rule are seen when judgement is given for the Wolf against the Sheep whose lamb has been stolen, and when the Ape employs all manner of unnatural creatures: '. . . Griffons, Minotaures, Crocodiles, Dragons, Beauers, and Centaures' (1123–4) to enforce his tyrannous usurpation. The situation is only resolved by divine intervention. Jove:

> The troubled kingdome of wilde beasts behelde,
> Whom not their kindly Souereigne did welde,
> But an vsurping Ape . . .

1231–3

—and sends Mercury to arouse the sleeping Lion to the proper exercise of his royalty. This is the central point of the poem, and Spenser extends the beast-allegory of the first part so as to avoid offence to the Queen, as well as to make the application of his moral universal.

'THE RUINES OF ROME'

This series of sonnets is a direct translation from Du Bellay. The theme of mourning over Rome's past glories is one that, as

163

we have seen, Spenser re-applies for his own original purpose in *The Ruines of Time*. This early work was probably written while Spenser was still at Cambridge.

'MUIOPOTMOS: OR THE FATE OF THE BUTTERFLIE'

This delightful poem can best be seen as a companion piece to *Virgils Gnat*, in which Spenser, accepting Virgil's authorship of *Culex* without question, extends his debt to the master's authority by writing an original work in the same vein. The story, of the proud and beautiful butterfly Clarion, who is caught and slain by the evil spider Aragnoll, is slight, and attempts to read it as a personal or political allegory (to which the request in the dedicatory letter to Lady Carey that she will 'make a milde construction' of the poem gives some justification) have not proved finally convincing.

But this is a poem which can be simply enjoyed. Spenser has enriched the slight framework of his story with every kind of delicious artifice. Like *Virgils Gnat*, the tone of the poem is mock-heroic:

> I sing of deadly dolorous debate,
> Stir'd vp through wrathfull *Nemesis* despight,
> Betwixt two mightie ones of great estate.

1—3

—and the description of the lovely Clarion arming himself for adventures abroad is a delicious parody of epic grandeur and convention:

> Vpon his head his glistering Burganet,
> The which was wrought by wonderous deuice,
> And curiously engrauen, he did set:
> The mettall was of rare and passing price;
> Not *Bilbo* steele, nor brasse from *Corinth* fet,
> Nor costly *Oricalche* from strange *Phoenice*;
> But such as could both *Phoebus* arrowes ward,
> And th'hayling darts of heauen beating hard.

73–80

Just as Spenser wrote *Muiopotmos* in the same vein as his translation of the Virgilian *Culex*, and *The Ruines of Time* in that of Du Bellay's *Antiquité*, so he accompanies his translations, *The Visions of Bellay* and *The Visions of Petrarch*, with his own *Visions of the Worlds Vanitie*. The form of a moralising sonnet, exemplifying the vulnerability of worldly glory, seems to have appealed strongly to him. It is probable that all these series are relatively early work, and that they were written partly as exercises: variations on a deeply engrossing theme: the *Visions* of Bellay and Petrarch are further examples of the same attitude and technique.

'DAPHNAIDA'

This elegy, published in 1591, is the saddest of all Spenser's poems, and the blackness of its melancholy is outstanding even among the elegiac writing of the time. On one level it can be seen as a kind of exploration of the melancholy that pervades *Complaints*. The occasion of the elegy is, however, pathetic enough. Douglas Howard (Daphne in her husband's poems: Spenser takes up the name), was the daughter of Henry, Lord Howard. She married Arthur Gorges in 1584, when she was thirteen, in the teeth of parental opposition. Their daughter, Ambrosia, was born two years later, and Douglas died in 1590 after a long and wretched illness at the age of eighteen.

Arthur Gorges himself was a poet: as such Spenser praises him in *Colin Clovts Come Home Againe*:

> And there is sad *Alcyon*, bent to mourne,
> Though fit to frame an euerlasting dittie,
> Whose gentle spright for *Daphnes* death doth tourn
> Sweet layes of loue to endlesse plaints of pittie.

384–7

That he was a poet probably explains why Spenser found the pastoral form particularly suitable to this elegy: Gorges, as Alcyon, is addressed as 'gentle shepheard'.

Daphnaida is strongly influenced by Chaucer's *Book of the Duchesse*, written on the occasion of the death of Blanche, first wife of John of Gaunt, Chaucer's patron. But whereas Chaucer evokes Blanche as she lived, the whole focus of *Daphnaida* is on Alcyon's grief, rather than on her whose loss has caused it:

> So doo I liue, so doo I daylie die,
> And pine away in selfe-consuming paine.

435-6

'COLIN CLOVTS COME HOME AGAINE'

This poem was published in 1595, together with *Astrophel* and other elegies by various hands lamenting Sidney's death. Spenser clearly regarded it as a sequel to *The Shepheardes Calender*, as the title shows. Themes from the earlier work are picked up: Hobbinol and Rosalind, the praise of the Queen, and various lines of satirical comment. The plan of the poem recalls the *September Eclogue*, where Hobbinol meets with Diggon on his return from a journey and hears his news. But *Colin Clovts Come Home Againe* is not an eclogue. Its setting is pastoral, but its matter is higher and more solemn in treatment than anything in the *Calender*. In the central passages, dealing with the Court, Spenser's idealising imagination, which was to find its true scope in *The Faerie Queene*, is combined with the harsh realism which is the basis of *Mother Hvbberds Tale*; and which is, indeed, the only starting point for true, complimentary idealism, as opposed to flattery.

'ASTROPHEL'

Astrophel, 'star lover', was the name Sidney took for himself as the lover of 'Stella' (star): Penelope Rich. Spenser retains it in the elegy, in which he presents Sidney's death, as the result of a wound received in battle, allegorically: Astrophel is slain by a wild boar, like Adonis, and he and Stella are transformed 'Into one flowre' (184). The mourning of Astrophel's fellow shepherds leads into the *Lay of Clorinda*, which was long thought to be by Sidney's sister, the Countess of Pembroke, but which appears to have been at least worked over by Spenser. It concludes with the conventional heavenly resolution:

> There liueth he in euerlasting blis,
> Sweet spirit neuer fearing more to die.

LAY OF CLORINDA 85-6

These were printed in one volume in 1595. It is unlikely that all the sonnets of *Amoretti* were written at one time, or that all were originally addressed to Elizabeth Boyle, whose marriage to Spenser is celebrated in the *Epithalamion*. It is possible that the form of the volume, which presents a sonnet sequence dealing with the vicissitudes of a courtship, crowned by a marriage-ode, is accidental: a pleasing fancy of the publisher, William Ponsonby. If so, he had an original mind: this is the only example of a sonnet sequence in English leading to such a conclusion. It seems more likely that Spenser collected existing sonnets, adding to their number with such an arrangement in mind. This would be in keeping with his conception of love, as creative and fruitful both physically and spiritually, and marriage, as sacramentally presenting this fulfilment. The figure of Charissa (Charity—*Faerie Queene* I, *10*), and the quest of Britomart which is to end in marriage, present the same essential image.

His use of sonnets written in praise of other beauties would be in keeping with this Platonic conception of Love, for in Elizabeth Boyle he saw a closer approximation to the Idea of Beauty itself than in all other women: all praise given to them was by right indirectly hers. As Donne says in *The Good Morrow*:

> But this, all pleasures fancies be,
> If ever any beauty I did see
> Which I desired and got, 'twas but a dreame of thee.

Spenser is in fact putting his earlier work to its proper purpose, now revealed to him in the beauty of his beloved.

The sonnets are in Spenser's own rhyme scheme, which appears occasionally elsewhere in his work: a strict variation of the 'Shakespearean' form (abab/bcbc/cdcd/ee). The sequence is made up of eighty-nine sonnets, with three lyric pieces at the end.

The sonnets themselves express the moods of the courtship at different stages. There is a definite progression from distant adoration to the intimacies of mutual and accepted love, with various vicissitudes on the way. The subject of the sonnets is love for a woman whose beauty and virtue show their divine origin. They deal not so much with this human revelation of beauty, as with the lover's reaction to it. Each sonnet presents a point of view, a part of the whole subject. The presentation of the actual, personal relationship is disciplined at every point by the appropriate conventions of thought and expression. (Spenser owes much to other writers, notably Desportes and Tasso, as well as Petrarch.)

This magnificent sequence is far too complex in its detail to examine closely, but certain points may be noted. The progress of the courtship is, like Colin's love in *The Shepheardes Calender*, linked to the passing of the seasons. At the opening it is spring:

> Then you faire flowre, in whom fresh youth doth raine,
> Prepare your selfe new loue to entertaine.   AMORETTI IV

Again, the penitential season of Lent has its parallel in the devotions of the lover:

> therefore, I lykewise on so holy day,
> for my sweet Saynt some seruice fit will find.   XXII

In the sixtieth sonnet he says his courtship has now lasted a year, and in the sixty-second hopes that the passing of winter may bring him grace:

> So likewise loue cheare you your heauy spright,
>   and chaunge old yeares annoy to new delight.

This year it is not Lent but Easter which suggests a more direct plea (this sonnet is often—disastrously—sung as a hymn):

> So let vs loue, deare loue, lyke as we ought,
>   loue is the lesson which the Lord vs taught.   LXVIII

Such an application of religion to love is not blasphemous: his love and service to his 'saint' is inspired by what is divine in her: it is not a distraction from his adoration of his Creator, but an aid to it.

The sequence ends on a minor tone, and the imagery is autumnal. Spenser laments his love's absence, 'Lyke as the Culuer on the bared bough' (LXXXIX). This melancholy conclusion, to be reversed by the triumph of the *Epithalamion*, is perhaps an effect of the convention by which sonnet sequences end, for the most part, either in rejection and despair, or, as in Petrarch's case, with the loss of the beloved through death: at least the loss of her physical presence.

One of the most interesting aspects of the courtship is Spenser's approach to his beloved. At first, he adores her from afar, over-awed by her beauty and right pride. He is her servant, not her equal. It is through his power, as a poet, to immortalise her transient manifestation of eternal beauty, that he attains her level:

> Faire be no lenger proud of that shall perish,
>> but that which shal you make immortall, cherish.   XXVII

This recalls the end of the *Epithalamion*, when he bids his song:

> Be vnto her a goodly ornament,
> And for short time an endlesse moniment.   432–3

The three lyrics at the end of the *Amoretti* provide a transition to the triumphant joy of the *Epithalamion*. They are slight, witty exercises, on the theme of Cupid's arrows, and recall the *March Eclogue*.

'EPITHALAMION'

The *Epithalamion* is without doubt the most glorious celebration of marriage in English. It is written within an established *genre*, for which there are many models in classical antiquity, notably in the work of Catullus and Theocritus. Spenser would also have been familiar with examples in French. Of all the traditions available to him he makes full use. It is interesting to compare this poem with the various *epithalamia* of other writers of the period, especially Herrick and Donne, a little later.

Spenser's inventive genius for devising verse forms here reaches its supreme triumph. He has developed a verse of eigh-teen lines, with the most complex orchestration of rhyme, and varying line lengths, and a refrain—'The woods shall to me answer and my Eccho ring'—subtly altered as the poem proceeds, tracing the progress of the wedding-day from dawn to night.

These were published in 1596 and are by far the most difficult of Spenser's poems. They can only be understood in the light of their Neo-Platonic sources, although many of the ideas in them are used elsewhere in Spenser's works, as has been seen.

The *Hymne in Honour of Love*, which praises Love as the generative force that brought the elements into harmony and created all living things, is written to celebrate Love's power over the poet, over whom he 'Doest tyrannize in euerie weaker part;' (4). This description of the suffering caused by Love recalls the presentation of Cupid in the House of Busyrane: mighty, but cruel. He goes on to say that, in the world created by Love's power, he operates still by infusing all creatures with desire for 'Beautie, borne of heauenly race' (112). And this is the cause of dreadful suffering:

> The whylst thou tyrant Loue doest laugh and scorne
> At their complaints, ...   134-5

It is clear, by reference to Spenser's treatment of Love elsewhere, that this Love is corrupted by its origins. The first impulse of desire is a perilous one, leading to fear and jealousy, and the rest of Cupid's train as this appears in the Masque in *The Faerie Queene* (III, *12*). Moreover, the end to which it leads is not Heavenly Beauty but: '. . . a Paradize Of all delight,' (280-1), which is seen not as a resting place, but as a final haven to be attained.

The *Hymne to Beautie* is the complement to its predecessor. It celebrates Venus, and her power of beauty, which infuses all forms in their degree and makes them desirable:

> Hath white and red in it such wondrous powre,
> That it can pierce through th'eyes vnto the hart,
> And therein stirre such rage and restless stowre,
> As nought but death can stint his dolours smart?   71-4

Here, again, the power celebrated is felt as being hurtful.

He goes on to show how lovers, with clearer sight, perceive the potential of the beloved's beauty, and this vision becomes for them actuality, so increasing their passion:

> Sometimes vpon her forhead they behold
> A thousand Graces masking in delight. 253–4

This idea is the philosophical basis of the exaggerated compliments paid by the sonneteers to their mistresses, examples of which can be found throughout Spenser's work, not least in his addresses to the Queen. But, again, there is no suggestion in this *Hymne* that the divine powers of Beauty should lead those who respond to it to its eternal origin in heaven.

The *Hymne of Heavenly Love* begins as one might expect from the context and the title:

> Loue, lift me vp vpon thy golden wings,
> From this base world vnto thy heauens hight. 1–2

Spenser then goes on to reject the doctrine of his previous *Hymnes*, made in 'th'heat of youth', deploring the ill effects they have had upon 'light wits'. He then proceeds to tell again how the world was made, but this time in specifically Christian terms. God, Who exists in love and in the mutual love of the Trinity:

> Yet being pregnant still with powrefull grace,
> And full of fruitfull loue. . . . 50–1

(these lines form the divine complement to Spenser's whole doctrine of human love elaborated in the *Epithalamion*), created the angels and, after Lucifer's rebellion, Man, whose Fall he redeemed by a supreme act of love in the Incarnation. The conclusion is that He alone is to be loved:

> Then shall thy rauisht soule inspired bee
> With heauenly thoughts, farre aboue humane skil,
> And thy bright radiant eyes shall plainely see
> Th'Idee of his pure glorie. 281–4

The implication is probably not that this love involves the rejection of created Beauty, but rather a just appreciation of the origins of that Beauty as a way to the 'Idea' of Beauty itself.

An Hymne of Heavenly Beautie certainly seems based on this concept. Spenser writes it, being:

> Rapt with the rage of mine own rauisht thought,
> Through contemplation of those goodly sights,
> And glorious images in heauen wrought,   I-3

—and he goes on to see celestial beauty in the whole variety of
the created universe; one may ascend from the earth through the
spheres of the physical heavens to Heaven itself, and there, rising
through the progressive glory of the angelic hierarchies, come at
last 'Before the footestoole of his Maiestie' (142). Spenser then
celebrates the attributes of Divinity: Righteousness, Truth, and
above all Wisdom, which is Divine understanding of God in all
His works, so transcending them:

> And looke at last vp to that soueraine light,
> From whose pure beams al perfect beauty springs,   295-6

It is possible that the juxtaposition of these two pairs of *Hymnes*
is deliberate, and that Spenser's 'repentance', expressed in the
dedication and at the opening of *Heavenly Love*, is purely conventional. I am myself inclined to think this; for nothing elsewhere in his work suggests he ever seriously held so imperfect
and inconclusive a view of love and beauty as is expressed in the
first two *Hymnes*. But this is only conjecture.

'PROTHALAMION'

The *Prothalamion* was composed in honour of the double marriage at Essex House of Lady Elizabeth and Lady Catherine
Somerset, daughters of Edward Somerset, Earl of Worcester. It
was published in 1596.

It is a beautiful poem: the structure of the verse is almost as
rich as that of the *Epithalamion*, and here again Spenser employs a
refrain: 'Sweete *Themmes* runne softly, till I end my Song.' By a
beautiful conceit, Spenser sees the two brides on their journey
down the river, as two swans:

> So purely white they were,
> That euen the gentle streame, the which them bare,
> Seem'd foule to them, and bad his billowes spare
> To wet their silken feathers, least they might
> Soyle their fayre plumes with water not so fayre,

And marre their beauties bright,
That shone as heauens light. . . .   46–52

The birds arrive at London, and here Spenser digresses in praise
of the city: 'my most kyndly Nurse,' (128), but more in grateful
memory of Leicester, to whose palace, now Essex House, the
brides have come. This passage has a twofold purpose. First it
provides a transition, by which the conceit of the swans can be
abandoned without disjunction, and also to give the full setting
for the noble wedding which he is celebrating. He emerges from
the pastoral convention into the more public mode of eulogy,
just as the brides leave their peaceful childhood for the responsibilities of noble marriage. For this reason, the praise accorded
to the city, and to Leicester, and most of all to Essex: 'That fillest
England with thy triumphs fame'—is fully in keeping with the
purpose of the poem. It is, naturally, not a personal poem, like
the *Epithalamion*. It is a formal celebration of a public event, and
the conventions Spenser uses are so disposed as to show the meaning and function of true marriage in this context.

Tail Piece

Spenser is not an easy poet, nor did he ever claim to be one. In
this book I have only tried to remove those accidental difficulties
in the way of enjoying his work which are the effect of time, of
whose action he was himself so cruelly aware. If I have succeeded,
then part of the debt I owe him for the delight his poetry affords
me is paid. If not, it is no fault of his, and I quote his own words
in apology both to him and to his readers:

> Of Faerie lond yet if he more inquire,
> By certaine signes here set in sundry place
> He may it find; ne let him then admire,
> But yield his sence to be too blunt and bace,
> That no'te without an hound fine footing trace.

FAERIE QUEENE II, Pro'. 4

Bibliography

I have divided this very brief book list into three parts: the text of Spenser's works, critical works relating to Spenser, and 16th-century texts of relevant interest.

TEXT

The most convenient edition of Spenser's works is:

The Poetical Works of Edmund Spenser ed. by J. C. Smith and E. Selincourt (Oxford). This includes all the poetry, together with all the dedications, the *Letter to Raleigh*, E.K.'s prefatory letter to *The Shepheardes Calender* and his General Argument, and the Spenser–Hervey correspondence, but not the *Veue of the Present State of Ireland* of which there is no readily attainable edition at present.

CRITICAL WORKS

The books suggested here are arranged in two categories: those dealing with Spenser's poetry and those of more general background interest.

Alistair Fowler: *Spenser and the Numbers of Time* (Routledge, 1964).

E. Greenlaw: *Studies in Spenser's Historical Allegory* (Johns Hopkins, Baltimore). This extremely useful book is out of print but is available at most libraries.

H. S. V. Jones: *A Spenser Handbook* (G. Bell and Sons Ltd). Most useful, with bibliographies for every aspect of Spenser's work.

M. P. Parker: *The Allegory of the Faerie Queene* (Oxford, 1960).

A Documentary History of Art, selected and edited by E. Holt, 2 vols. (Doubleday, Anchor PB, 1958).

J. Burckhardt: *The Civilisation of the Renaissance in Italy*, trans. Middlemore, 2 vols. (Harper Torch Books, PB, 1958).

C. S. Lewis: *The Allegory of Love* (Oxford, 1936). There is also a paperback edition in Galaxy Books (Oxford).

C. S. Lewis: *The Discarded Image* (Cambridge, 1964).

A. O. Lovejoy: *The Great Chain of Being* (Harper Torch Books, PB).

Edgar Wind: *Pagan Mysteries in the Renaissance* (Faber, 1958).

OTHER TEXTS

Sir Philip Sidney: *Astrophel and Stella*, published in *Silver Poets of the Sixteenth Century*, which includes also the poems of Sir Walter Raleigh and Sir John Davies's *Orchestra*. Ed. by G. Bullett (Everyman PB, 1935).

Sir Philip Sidney: *Apologie for Poetrie*, ed. by J. Churton Collins (Oxford, 1907).

Index